CHUCK PETERS
JANA MAGRUDER
STEPHANIE SALVATORE

FLIP the
SCRIPT

DISRUPTING TRADITION FOR
THE SAKE OF THE NEXT GENERATION

© 2022 Lifeway Christian Resources
Reprinted March 2023

Item 005842461
ISBN 978-1-0877-8520-2

Published by Lifeway Christian Resources
200 Powell Place, Suite 100
Brentwood, TN 37027—7707

For ordering or inquiries, visit www.lifeway.com, or write
Lifeway Christian Resources Customer Service
200 Powell Place, Suite 100
Brentwood, TN 37027-7707

We believe that the Bible has God for its author; salvation for its end; and truth, without any mixture of error, for its matter and that all Scripture is totally true and trustworthy. To review Lifeway's doctrinal guideline, please visit lifeway.com/doctrinalguideline.

FOREWORD

Invite people into your life, not to a location.

A church planter once shared those words with me, and it radically impacted the way I view evangelism. Upon reflection, I'm not sure why the idea was eye-opening. After all, Jesus clearly modeled the importance of building relationships every time He said yes to eating with tax collectors and sinners. The Master Teacher was first a Master Relationship-Builder.

How do we reach people today? It's the right question, and it's answered carefully inside this book. In a secularized society, relationships are the way forward, and no relationships are more powerful than those forged in the kids and student ministries. I urge you to listen carefully to Chuck Peters and his team as they unpack the philosophy that informed Lifeway's newest line of curriculum, Hyfi. *Flip the Script* explains the simple shifts that we must make in order to pass the baton to the next generation. I could not be prouder of this team, who labored countless hours to create this. I could not be more thrilled to offer these tools to the next wave of church leaders.

Ben Mandrell

President & CEO
Lifeway Christian Resources

ABOUT THE AUTHORS

Chuck, Jana, and Stephanie have worked together for almost a decade. They share a deep love for the church and Kids Ministry and are committed to finding creative and accessible ways for leaders to share the gospel with the next generation. Among their favorite projects together are concepting the ETCH NextGen Ministry Conference, ideating annual VBS themes, developing Explore The Bible: Kids, and creating The Gospel Project story circle and timeline. A little more about them—

Chuck Peters is the Director of Lifeway Kids. He is a graduate of Columbia Bible College. Before his role at Lifeway, Chuck had a prolific career in television and video production; an adventure that took him from his home state of New Jersey to Northern California, Central Florida, and then Nashville. He is a 3-time Emmy Award Winning producer, writer, and on-screen talent. Chuck and his wife, Cris, have served in Student and Children's Ministry vocationally and as volunteers for many years. They have four amazing children: Tally, Tristen, Tyson, and Tate.

Jana Magruder serves as the Strategic Initiatives Director of Lifeway Kids. With a background in education, publishing, and ministry, she loves championing the local church to help families disciple kids of all ages. She is a Baylor graduate and the author of *Nothing Less* and *Kids Ministry that Nourishes*. Jana and her husband, Michael, are native Texans planted in Tennessee and love to explore both states with their three kids: Morgan Grace, Jason, and Nicholas.

Stephanie Salvatore serves as the Creative Director for Lifeway Kids and has a passion for finding out-of-the-box solutions to any creative problem. She designed for a variety of publishing mediums (from magazine design to app development) and ages (from student ministry to senior adults) before discovering a passion for kids ministry. Hailing originally from New York and northern Indiana, Stephanie now lives in Tennessee with her husband Joe and two teenagers, Ben and Chloe.

ACKNOWLEDGMENTS

There are many amazing thought leaders who have spoken into *Flip the Script*. Without them, this project would not have been possible. We would like to thank:

Scott McConnell, Executive Director of Lifeway Research, worked to get us the data that served as the anchor for this story. We are grateful for his expertise and guidance in incorporating strong research that supports the urgent calls for action represented in each chapter.

The Publishing Team: Kayla Stevens, Publishing Team Leader, served as our content editor and helped weave and craft two years' worth of scribbles and notes gleaned from hundreds of hours we spent together working on models, frameworks, and writing. Jeremy Carroll, Publishing Manager, oversaw all of the steps of the publishing process on an expedited schedule. Isaac Kierstead, digital content editor, contributed kids ministry expertise from the local church.

Lifeway Students Team: Ben Trueblood, Director of Lifeway Students, gave incredible insight into the world of today's teenagers, including his own valuable research in his book *Within Reach* that is quoted multiple times in *Flip the Script*. John Paul Basham and Drew Dixon have been at the table with us from the beginning, offering wisdom for working with students.

Team West: Crystal Mazzuca, Heidi Hensley, Johnny Rogers, Kai Vilhelmsen, and Lauren Jackson taught us so much as our subject matter experts who work tirelessly in NextGen ministry in their local churches in the West.

Special thanks to Ben and Lynley Mandrell. This all began with your encouragement to walk alongside churches as they seek to live on mission and reach their neighbors in post-Christian areas. Thank you for your vision, support, and encouragement!

WE ARE GRATEFUL FOR EACH OF YOU AND THE GIFTS YOU BROUGHT TO THIS LABOR OF LOVE. TOGETHER, LET'S CONTINUE TO FLIP THE SCRIPT FOR SUCH A TIME AS THIS.

1

WE'RE READING FROM AN OLD SCRIPT

THE PROBLEM:
As church attendance and membership wanes, Judeo-Christian beliefs are becoming less and less ingrained in American culture. Kids and students are growing up with a foundationally secular worldview that tells them the meaning of life is to define themselves. The pressure to do this has resulted in unprecedented levels of anxiety, loneliness, and a desperate need to belong. This secular framework makes it harder and harder for kids to hear and relate to biblical teaching.

3

FLIP THE SCRIPT: FROM SEEN TO KNOWN

THIS MODEL MEETS THE CULTURAL NEED FOR BELONGING:
Belonging means more than just helping kids feel seen. Extravagant welcome is needed to truly help them feel known. We must have intentional strategies that move kids and students from feeling like outsiders to a place of safety and comfort, where they can begin to participate and learn. Relationships with friends, leaders, influencers, and pastors help open ears to the gospel and truly connect newcomers to the church.

2

FLIP THE SCRIPT: FROM "HEAR" TO "HERE"

A NEW MINISTRY MODEL IS NEEDED:
The church hasn't been effective in answering this cultural crisis. We've mistakenly assumed kids and students are starting with a Christian framework. A new ministry model is needed: one that doesn't assume kids and students arrive ready to learn; one that doesn't assume a church background; one that meets the big cultural need for belonging and answers the big cultural question of identity.

THIS MODEL ANSWERS THE CULTURAL QUESTION OF IDENTITY:
Teaching content focused on biblical identity answers the big cultural question "Who am I?" Twelve identity statements (such as *I am known*, *I am secure*, *I am here for a purpose*) teach kids and students they can know who they are when they know who God is. Their identity is defined by who God is.

THIS MODEL WORKS FOR THE WHOLE CHURCH:
The whole church should get behind these strategies, not only because of the outcomes for kids and students, but also because they are transferable to the whole church! Churches should be intentional about moving outsiders into the church, helping all people build relationship networks, and making relationship-rich environments the central hub of the church.

We need to hold tightly to Jesus alone, not our ministry models. As times change, we must be willing to allow our ministry strategies to flex to meet people where they are.

Culture may change over time, but some things are timeless. We must always teach what matters. We must always teach the Bible with sound doctrine to reach the heart of a child, to both learn and respond.

WE'RE READING
FROM AN OLD SCRIPT

FLIPPING THE SCRIPT: A FRESH PERSPECTIVE

Imagine you've been asked to close your eyes and explain to someone how to run. You think for a minute, then close your eyes and call out, "First, take a deep breath. Then, lift your left knee. OK, now propel your left foot forward and put it on the ground."

You're frustrated when your confused trainee argues with you. "Take a deep breath? Lift my *what*? What are you talking about? Why would I need this?" You open your eyes to discover you've been explaining how to run ... to a fish. You've assumed you and the fish have shared life experiences related to things *you never even think about*—oxygen, gravity, and knees! Because of that, your explanation has fallen on deaf ears. (Do fish even have ears?)

In this rapidly changing world, talking to kids and students about spiritual things can feel a little bit like explaining the mechanics of running to a fish. We assume a shared understanding of how the world works, and they stare back at us with gills sucking water, swish their fins, and swim on. We need to change our viewpoint—to climb into the fishbowl alongside kids and students and look out at the world from their perspective. The view may feel warped to us, but it can help us learn how to reach this generation in a way they understand.

It's time to admit that we are reading from an old script. We are communicating the timeless truth of the gospel with old strategies that aren't connecting with younger generations anymore. We need to flip the script!

CHURCH ATTENDANCE IS FALLING

In 2021, The American National Family Life Survey analyzed how often people attended religious services while growing up. While Gen X, Baby Boomers, and the Silent Generation reported weekly church attendance at more than 50%, the majority of Millennials and Gen Z did not grow up attending church weekly.[1]

58% 57% 52% 45% 40%

SILENT GENERATION BABY BOOMERS GENERATION X MILLENNIALS GENERATION Z

Fewer than half of Millennials and Gen Z attended church weekly while growing up.

You never really understand
a person until you consider
things from his point of view
… until you climb into his skin
and walk around in it.

—Atticus Finch
To Kill a Mockingbird

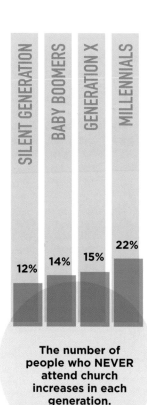

SILENT GENERATION 12%
BABY BOOMERS 14%
GENERATION X 15%
MILLENNIALS 22%

The number of people who NEVER attend church increases in each generation.

While the American National Family Life Survey looked at church attendance *while growing up*, a 2019 Pew study asked each generation about their *current church attendance*, and the numbers in younger generations were even more dismal. Only 22% of Millennials reported weekly church attendance. That number bumps up to just 35% if you add in the number of Millennials who attend services once or twice per month. Furthermore, the number of Millennials who *never* attend services (22%) is the same as those who attend weekly. Church attendance looked marginally better for Generation X, with 32% reporting weekly attendance, and 46% reporting attendance at once per month or more.[2]

Since most parents of teenagers and kids fall into these two generations, it is reasonable to conclude that less than 50% of NextGen kids are attending church once per month or more.

FEWER PEOPLE ARE IDENTIFYING AS CHRISTIAN

When it comes to identifying themselves as Christians, fewer and fewer people in each generation do so.

According to Pew Research, Christians are reporting church attendance at the same rate as they did in 2009. They explain, "The nation's overall rate of religious attendance is declining not because Christians are attending church less often, but rather because there are now fewer Christians as a share of the population."[3]

While more than eight in ten in the Silent Generation identify themselves as Christians, the numbers decline with each successive generation. Millennials are the first generation in America in which Christians are a minority, with just 49% identifying as such. We can expect that if the parents of Gen Z are not identifying as Christians, it is less likely their children and grandchildren will.[4]

IN EACH GENERATION, IDENTIFYING AS A CHRISTIAN AND CHURCH ATTENDANCE IS DECREASING.

84% IDENTIFY AS A CHRISTIAN

61% ATTEND ONCE PER MONTH OR MORE

76% IDENTIFY AS A CHRISTIAN

49% ATTEND ONCE PER MONTH OR MORE

67% IDENTIFY AS A CHRISTIAN

46% ATTEND ONCE PER MONTH OR MORE

49% IDENTIFY AS A CHRISTIAN

35% ATTEND ONCE PER MONTH OR MORE

SILENT GENERATION
(1928-1945)

BABY BOOMERS
(1946-1964)

GENERATION X
(1965-1980)

MILLENNIALS
(1981-1996)

1948—2009: CHURCH MEMBERSHIP DECLINED 15 PERCENTAGE POINTS

2009—2020: CHURCH MEMBERSHIP DECLINED 14 PERCENTAGE POINTS

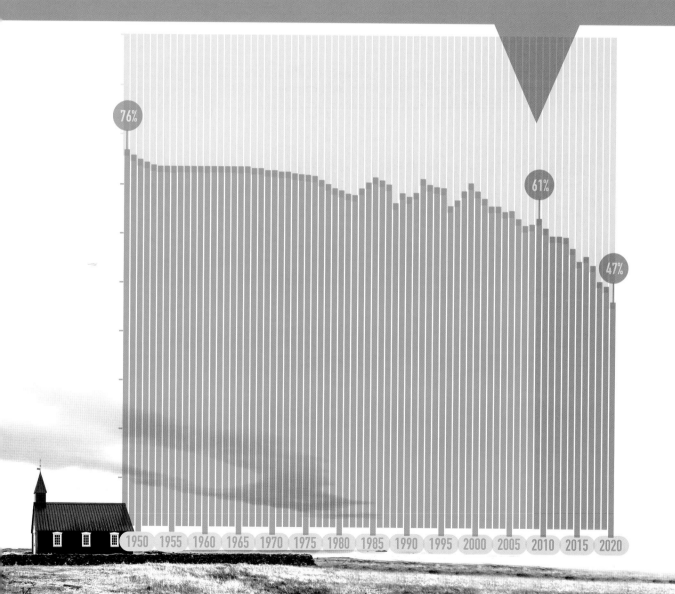

76%

61%

47%

1950 1955 1960 1965 1970 1975 1980 1985 1990 1995 2000 2005 2010 2015 2020

CHURCH MEMBERSHIP IS DROPPING AT AN ACCELERATED PACE

With the number of people who identify as Christians declining, it's no surprise that church membership in the U.S. is lower as well. In 1948, 76% of Americans reported being a member of a church, synagogue, or mosque. That number has now dipped below 50%. Note that it took 61 years to drop 15 percentage points and just 11 years to drop another 14 percentage points. We recognize that 2020 was an anomaly of church statistics during the start of the COVID-19 pandemic. But, even without taking 2020 into account, the percentages of church membership are falling at an alarming pace.[5]

These statistics paint a bleak picture for Christians and seem to point to a disconnect between the church and people they are trying to reach. Certainly church attendance and membership don't guarantee saving faith in Jesus, but they *can* indicate to what degree religious values and ideas are shaping culture. Let's step back and look through the wider historical lens at church attendance and its effect on culture and worldview.

At one time, church was the center of society. Churches were built as the centerpiece of a city, and city life revolved around them. Baptisms, marriages, funerals, and festivals provided the foundation of community life. There was social benefit, and even social pressure, to belong to a religious community. For some people and communities this represented true saving faith, and for others it was merely institutional or cultural. Both believers and non-believers had similar ideas about how the world worked that were based on Judeo-Christian ideas. Most of society agreed on things like the existence of God, good and evil, heaven and hell, and most issues of morality and social ethics.

As church attendance and membership have declined, the church has moved to the periphery of public life. As its influence over public discourse and policy has weakened, ideas that have no spiritual basis have replaced religion as the key influencer of public life.

(WE HAVE SHIFTED) FROM A SOCIETY IN WHICH IT WAS VIRTUALLY IMPOSSIBLE NOT TO BELIEVE IN GOD, TO ONE IN WHICH FAITH, EVEN FOR THE STAUNCHEST BELIEVER, IS ONE HUMAN POSSIBILITY AMONG OTHERS.

—CHARLES TAYLOR
PHILOSOPHER,
SECULARISM EXPERT

SECULARISM'S INFLUENCE ON WORLDVIEW

The dominant worldview of any population is the aggregate of the ideals of individuals. As increasing numbers of people turn away from faith and faith communities, the result is an increasing separation between religion and public life. In America today, secularism (attitudes/activities that have no religious or spiritual basis) has replaced the church in many contexts as the primary driver of culture.

As society has become more secular, belief in God has moved from being expected to being unchallenged to being just one option among others.[6] Every aspect of society is influenced by secular ideas. Education, literature, and entertainment answer questions like "What is the meaning of life? How does the universe work? How do we know right from wrong?" in ways that are no longer shaped primarily by religious beliefs.

Christian parents may try to shield their children from a secular worldview, but it's pervasive. It is in every facet of society, including our churches. With access to the internet, kids today are global citizens who encounter a myriad of belief systems at younger and younger ages. In entertainment and online, belief systems aren't presented in an organized way that might lead kids and students to consider whether or not they agree, but rather as an assumption that *everyone* believes in moral relativism, new age, astrology, self help, or nothing at all. Christian belief systems that are perceived by some as restricting freedom in any way are (at best) undermined with jokes couched as entertainment or (at worst) openly mocked.

How do we engage a generation of unchurched and underchurched kids and students to whom truths and stories in Scripture are unknown and the topics, people, and places seem foreign? Moreover, how do we engage a generation in which the very fabric of what they believe to be true about how the world works is counter to Christian teachings? Let's begin by understanding exactly what this generation DOES believe.

ATHEISM AND AGNOSTICISM ARE ON THE RISE IN YOUNGER GENERATIONS

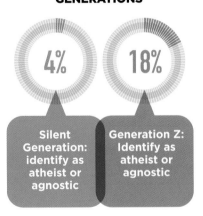

4%

18%

Silent Generation: identify as atheist or agnostic

Generation Z: Identify as atheist or agnostic

Not only do 34% of Generation Z identify as religiously unaffiliated, they are also more likely to identify as atheist or agnostic than any other generation.

The Christian family,
Christian church, and
Christian school must
not assume that the next
generations will accept
the conclusions that
seem so obvious to
older generations.

—Kevin DeYoung

THESE SEVEN BELIEFS ARE AT THE CORE OF EXPRESSIVE INDIVIDUALISM

1

The highest good is individual freedom, happiness, self-definition and self-expression.

2

Traditions, religions, received wisdom, regulations, and social ties that restrict individual freedom, happiness, self-definition, and self-expression must be reshaped, deconstructed, or destroyed.

3

The world will inevitably improve as the scope of individual freedom grows. Technology—in particular the internet—will motor this progression toward utopia.

4

The primary social ethic is tolerance of everyone's self-defined quest for individual freedom and self-expression. Any deviation from this ethic of tolerance is dangerous and must not be tolerated. Therefore social justice is less about economic or class inequality and more about issues of equality relating to individual identity, self-expression and personal autonomy.

5

Humans are inherently good.

6

Large-scale structures and institutions are suspicious at best and evil at worst.

7

Forms of external authority are rejected and personal authenticity is lauded.

WHAT EXACTLY IS TODAY'S WORLDVIEW?

Today's worldview is primarily shaped by *expressive individualism*, a term coined by philosopher Robert Bellah.[7] Yuval Levin in *The Fractured Republic* describes it like this:

> (Expressive individualism) suggests not only a desire to pursue one's own path but also a yearning for fulfillment through the definition and articulation of one's own identity. It is a drive both to be more like whatever you already are and also to live in society by fully asserting who you are. The capacity of individuals to define the terms of their own existence by defining their personal identities is increasingly equated with liberty and with the meaning of some of our basic rights, and it is given pride of place in our self-understanding.[8]

For the most part, expressive individualism rejects anything external (values or duties defined by society, religion, or previous generations). It encourages defining one's "self" internally and expressing that self-created identity to the world. It layers on additional pressure that you don't just have the *right* to do this, but you have the *responsibility* to do this. Anything that restricts your freedom must be eliminated. There is no external definition of right and wrong. All definitions revolve around you and your fulfillment. The ultimate goal of this worldview is not to adhere or listen to outside standards but to be authentic to the standards you've identified for yourself. Should you look outside of yourself? Absolutely, but only to defend the rights of those whose definitions of "self" have been marginalized. You *must* defend their right to define themselves and express that definition.

In *The Disappearing Church*, Mark Sayers offers a list of seven core beliefs that reflect an expressive individualist society.[9] Remember our fish analogy? As you read the seven beliefs, remember that **this** is the world our kids and students see when they are looking out through the lens of their secular fishbowl.

HOW PERVASIVE IS EXPRESSIVE INDIVIDUALISM?

Your city and your church are influenced, to some degree, by expressive individualism and post-Christian philosophy. This thinking dominates the culture and public discourse in some areas of the country and has a moderate influence in other areas.

In 2019, Barna research measured post-Christian beliefs across the U.S. based on 16 measurements of belief, identity, and practice. To qualify as "post-Christian," individuals had to meet 9 or more of the 16 measurements. The results are wide-ranging. The highest ranking post-Christian cities are in Springfield and Holyoke, MA scoring at 66%, while Charleston and Huntington, WV scored only 32% as post-Christian.[10]

Regardless of where you live in the country, the kids and students you serve live in a global world, and they are most certainly being influenced by post-Christian thought. Are you seeing any of the following viewpoints among kids and students?

- They feel that "Jesus is the only way" seems intolerant.
- They challenge that the biblical teaching about binary gender is bigoted and unsafe.
- They talk about themselves as a "brand."
- They refer to "my truth" rather than "the truth."
- They make decisions by "following their heart" or "tapping into an inner power."
- They celebrate others regardless of behavior.
- They struggle in situations where they are asked to give up their own preferences/rights for the good of the group.
- They struggle with the idea that humans are sinful by nature.
- They believe personal happiness and fulfillment are the meaning of life.
- They view equality in terms of defending people's freedom of expression and self-definitions rather than in economic terms.

SECULARISM HAS A STRONG FOOTHOLD IN AMERICAN CULTURE

60%

60% of Americans agree that religious belief is a matter of personal opinion; it is not about objective truth.

66%

66% of American agree that everyone sins a little, but most people are good by nature.

WHICH CITIES RANK AS THE MOST "POST-CHRISTIAN?"

#	City	%	#	City	%	#	City	%
1	Springfield-Holyoke, MA	66%	36	Pittsburgh, PA	47%	70	Dayton, OH	38%
2	Portland-Auburn, ME	60%	37	Wilmington, NC	47%	71	Cincinnati, OH	38%
3	Providence, RI-New Bedford, MA	59%	38	San Diego, CA	46%	72	Atlanta, GA	38%
4	Burlington, VT	59%	39	Las Vegas, NV	46%	73	Norfolk-Portsmouth-Newport News, VA	38%
5	Boston, MA-Manchester, NH	57%	40	Cedar Rapids-Waterloo, IA	46%	74	Raleigh-Durham-Fayetteville, NC	38%
6	Albany-Schenectady-Troy, NY	56%	41	Syracuse, NY	46%	75	Colorado Springs-Pueblo, CO	37%
7	Hartford-New Haven, CT	56%	42	Spokane, WA	45%	76	Ft. Wayne, IN	37%
8	Rochester, NY	55%	43	Harlingen-Weslaco-Brownsville-McAllen, TX	45%	77	San Antonio, TX	36%
9	Santa Barbara-Santa Maria-San Luis Obispo, CA	54%	44	Miami-Ft. Lauderdale, FL	45%	78	Ft. Smith-Fayetteville-Springdale-Rogers, AR	36%
10	Seattle-Tacoma, WA	54%	45	Flint-Saginaw-Bay City, MI	45%	79	Traverse City-Cadillac, MI	36%
11	Madison, WI	54%	46	Baltimore, MD	45%	80	Paducah, KY-Cape Girardeau, MO-Harrisburg-Mt. Vernon, IL	36%
12	Wilkes Barre-Scranton-Hazelton, PA	54%	47	Phoenix-Prescott, AZ	44%	81	South Bend-Elkhart, IN	36%
13	Buffalo, NY	53%	48	Minneapolis-St. Paul, MN	44%	82	Oklahoma City, OK	35%
14	Ft. Myers-Naples, FL	52%	49	Orlando-Daytona Beach-Melbourne, FL	44%	83	Grand Rapids-Kalamazoo-Battle Creek, MI	35%
15	Davenport-Rock Island-Moline, IL	52%	50	Peoria-Bloomington, IL	44%	84	Savannah, GA	35%
16	Tuscon-Sierra Vista, AZ	51%	51	Waco-Temple-Bryan, TX	43%	85	Jacksonville, FL	34%
17	San Francisco-Oakland-San Jose, CA	50%	52	Green Bay-Appleton, WI	43%	86	Lansing, MI	34%
18	Reno, NV	50%	53	Johnstown-Altoona-St. College, PA	43%	87	Indianapolis, IN	34%
19	Chico-Redding, CA	50%	54	Portland, OR	42%	88	Columbia, SC	34%
20	New York, NY	50%	55	Albuquerque-Santa Fe, NM	42%	89	Charleston, SC	34%
21	Monterey-Salinas, CA	49%	56	West Palm Beach-Ft. Pierce, FL	42%	90	Dallas-Ft. Worth, TX	33%
22	Philadelphia, PA	49%	57	Wausau-Rhinelander, WI	42%	91	Corpus Christi, TX	33%
23	Sacramento-Stockton-Modesto, CA	48%	58	Milwaukee, WI	42%	92	Kansas City, KS-MO	33%
24	Boise, ID	48%	59	Columbus, OH	42%	93	Mobile, AL-Pensacola-Ft. Walton Beach, FL	33%
25	Austin, TX	48%	60	Yakima-Pasco-Richland-Kennewick, WA	41%	94	Richmond-Petersburg, VA	33%
26	Des Moines-Ames, IA	48%	61	Lincoln-Hastings-Kearney, NE	41%	95	Harrisburg-Lancaster-Lebanon-York, PA	33%
27	Chicago, IL	48%	62	Tampa-St. Petersburg-Sarasota, FL	41%	96	Salt Lake City, UT	32%
28	Detroit, MI	48%	63	Youngstown-Warren, OH	41%	97	Wichita-Hitchinson-Dodge City-Salina-Manhattan, KS	32%
29	Washington, DC-Haggerstown, MD	48%	64	Eugene, OR	40%	98	Baton Rouge, LA	32%
30	Los Angeles, CA	47%	65	St. Louis, MO	40%	99	Knoxville, TN	32%
31	Fresno-Visalia, CA	47%	66	El Paso, TX	39%	100	Charleston-Huntington, WV	32%
32	Denver, CO	47%	67	Cleveland-Akron-Canton, OH	39%			
33	Sioux Falls-Mitchell, SD	47%	68	Houston, TX	38%			
34	Omaha, NE	47%	69	Champaign-Springfield-Decatur, IL	38%			
35	Toledo, OH	47%						

WHO IS GEN Z?
(BORN 1997-2012)

Market Research firm, McKinsey & Company, helps companies appeal to specific target audiences. Here are several ways the search for "truth" drives the overall behavior of Generation Z:

IDENTITY NOMADS
Don't define themselves in only one way

They want to express personal truth.

COMMUNAHOLIC
Feel radically inclusive of people/groups

They want to connect through different truths.

DIALOGUER
Desire fewer confrontations, more dialogue

They want to understand different truths.

MENTAL HEALTH SNAPSHOTS

53% of Gen Z (ages 13-25) reported that the biggest challenge they faced during the pandemic was their mental health.

61% of Gen Z (ages 13-25) say adults in their lives don't truly know the extent of their struggles.

48% of Gen Z (ages 13-25) say they are moderately or extremely depressed.

21% of Gen Z (ages 13-25) say they are extremely lonely.

MORE THAN HALF
of Gen Z adults (ages 18-22) identified with 10 out of 11 feelings associated with loneliness.

"MY MENTAL HEALTH IS FAIR TO POOR"

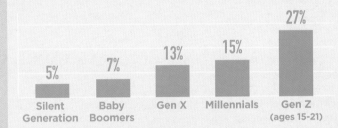

Silent Generation	Baby Boomers	Gen X	Millennials	Gen Z (ages 15-21)
5%	7%	13%	15%	27%

GEN Z FEELS STRESS ABOUT THE NEWS

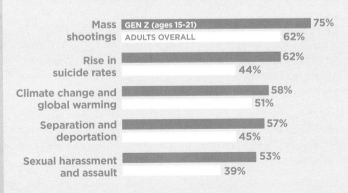

	GEN Z (ages 15-21)	ADULTS OVERALL
Mass shootings	75%	62%
Rise in suicide rates	62%	44%
Climate change and global warming	58%	51%
Separation and deportation	57%	45%
Sexual harassment and assault	53%	39%

THE PROBLEM OF EXPRESSIVE INDIVIDUALISM

The philosophy of expressive individualism puts tremendous pressure on children. Imagine the pressure that comes with defining "self," rights, and ethics—on kids and students whose brains are not yet fully developed. And that pressure doesn't end with defining themselves. Once they define themselves by looking within themselves, there is additional pressure to express, defend, find people who celebrate that definition, and reject those who disagree.

Even before the global pandemic of 2020 forced kids into social isolation, studies show that this generation experience the highest rates of loneliness and depression. Two years into the pandemic, 53% of Gen Z report that the biggest challenge they faced during this time was their mental health. In addition, 48% say that they are moderately to extremely depressed. A separate study concludes that Gen Z adults identified with 10 out of 11 feelings associated with loneliness."[11]

Some might point to the rise in phone or screen use and growing up in a hyper-connected world as the source of the mental health crisis. Others may point to the effects of isolation during the pandemic. Others point to things like the rise in school shootings, political rancor, or economic stress. Certainly these play a role. But the fact is, we weren't created to define ourselves or to be the center of all things. The impact of growing up in a culture obsessed with "self" impacts mental health.

Creating self-definition ends ultimately in a performative lifestyle. The millennial actress, Zendaya, exhorts young people to "... just try hard to be you."[12] This statement seems ridiculous to older generations who don't consider "being you" to be a performance that requires hard work. But it resonates deeply with younger generations who live daily with the pressure to act out the identity they've created.

... JUST
TRY HARD
TO BE YOU.
—ZENDAYA, ACTRESS

VOICES IN CULTURE

Whatever choice you make, let it come from your heart.
—Queen Clarice in *Princess Diaries 2: Royal Engagement*

The rest of the world may follow the rules, but I must follow my heart.
—Ernesto de la Cruz from *Coco*

Life doesn't give us purpose. We give life purpose.
—The Flash (DC Comics)

If you feel like you really want to define yourself, and you have the ability to articulate those parameters and that in itself defines you, then do it.
—Kristen Stewart, actress

It's time to see what I can do
To test the limits and break through
No right, no wrong, no rules for me
I'm free.
— "Let It Go" lyrics from *Frozen*

I've always been fascinated by the idea that there's no such thing as evil; it's all in your point of view.
— Eli Roth, film director

There is additional pressure to avoid getting caught accidentally stepping outside of one's created definition. Attackers are always watchful to "out" a hypocrite who steps out of line. Kids and students feel the pressure to hide behind the cover story of what they've created. They sense this cover story is a fraud because they sense they were made for something different. And when your whole identity is a performance you've invented, it leads to isolation, fear, fragility, and exhaustion.

An invented identity is fluid. What happens to the child who, after time passes, questions that definition? If that definition turns out to be wrong, she only has herself to blame. As they grow, kids and students are confronted with a continual need to define themselves over and over because they can't find fulfillment from their sense of "self." When the thing they wanted most isn't fulfilling, what follows is loneliness and confusion about an identity built on fluidity and feelings.

Whatever path you decide to take in this life, be true to yourself.
—Yu Shu Lien in *Crouching Tiger Hidden Dragon*

You just be and you don't let anyone tell you who you are. You don't need labels to make yourself feel valuable, you're better than that.
—PewDiePie, Swedish YouTuber

Your self-worth is determined by you. You don't have to depend on someone else telling you who you are.
—Beyoncé Knowles, singer

If [it] come[s] from inside you, [it's] always [the] right one.
—Mr. Miyagi in *The Karate Kid*

I believe everyone is looking for the answers, but the answers are within ourselves.
—Miranda Kerr, model

Fairy Tales can come true. You just gotta make them happen. It all depends on you.
—Tiana in *The Princess and the Frog*

THE PROBLEM OF BEING HEARD AND UNDERSTOOD

The current framework of expressive individualism is incompatible with Christian teachings, so we have an intellectual problem to overcome when talking to kids and students about spiritual things. But before we can even address the problem of understanding, we have to deal with the fact that giving up your life to find it (see Matthew 16:25) doesn't sound like good news to students and kids whose highest values are self-definition and self-expression. This message sounds threatening to kids whose worldview tells them happiness depends on self-fulfillment. If you reject or dismiss the identity they've worked so hard to create, their worldview says your words and beliefs must be unsafe; therefore, you must be unsafe. External authority, and especially that given by an institution, is viewed by many kids and students as coercive, intrusive, and suspicious.

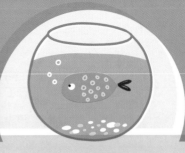

WORLDVIEW THEN

Most peers identified as Christian, attended church regularly, and shared values rooted in religious ideals.

In general, culture believed the meaning of life was *TO BE GOOD.*

Believed rights and ethics were defined by external sources— government, religion, society, family. The world improved as people behaved morally. Society should help the economically or socially disadvantaged.

Understanding the gospel was a matter of **connecting the dots** of existing beliefs.

WORLDVIEW NOW

Most peers do NOT identify as Christian, attend church regularly, or share values rooted in religious ideals.

In general, culture now believes the meaning of life is *TO DEFINE MYSELF.*

Believe rights and ethics are defined internally, with no external authority. The world improves as personal freedom grows. Society must defend those whose identity is marginalized.

Existing beliefs contradict the gospel. We will need to **draw new dots.**

The only way to overcome this suspicion is by awakening a longing to connect. Kids are not going to be able to hear what you have to say until they determine you are trustworthy. You can't assume their trust just by showing up—you'll need to work to earn the right to be heard. Kids and students will need to feel a sense of belonging and psychological safety before you can move forward to address the issue of understanding the gospel.

In terms of helping kids move toward an understanding of gospel truths, the idea of sin sounds like nonsense to those who believe people are inherently good. Eternal life is irrelevant to someone who doesn't believe in heaven. Submission to Christ sounds dangerous to someone who worships the self as ultimate authority. Tim Keller describes the problem like this:

> For a thousand years … the culture created people who had the basic "furniture" for a Christian worldview. They usually believed in a personal God, they often believed in an afterlife, heaven and hell. They believed they should be "good" and they weren't perfect, and that they therefore did need forgiveness. So you could call those the "religious dots"—belief in God, belief in an afterlife, belief in a moral law, belief in sin. The church could assume that people would just show up in church. If they came they would have a general respect for the Bible, and they would have some basic understanding of these things, and evangelism was just waiting for people to show up and then connecting the dots. [13]

But, what do you do if the dots don't exist? How do you reach a generation that is suspicious of the church? What happens when you talk to a kid or a student about heaven, Jesus, or his need for salvation—but he doesn't believe in heaven, he's never heard of Jesus, and he disagrees that he is a sinner who needs this Jesus?

In 2021, Lifeway Research asked about issues important to the American public. The categories of "peace," "hope," and "purpose and fulfillment" all ranked higher than "certainty I will go to heaven." These findings reinforce the idea that the

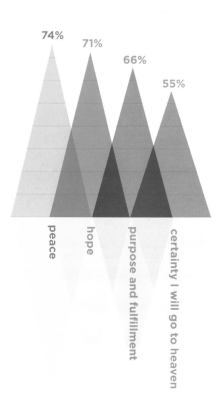

"IN MY LIFE, IT'S VERY IMPORTANT TO HAVE … "

74% peace
71% hope
66% purpose and fulfillment
55% certainty I will go to heaven

previous dots may not be there anymore. Only 55% of all those surveyed ranked certainty of eternal life as "very important." That percentage dropped to 40% of 18-34 year olds.[14] In a separate study, 47% of non-religious people said they *never* wonder if they will go to heaven when they die.[15]

The Campus Crusade style of initiative evangelism of the 1950s-1980s was successful because it clearly connected the dots of pre-existing beliefs in moral law and eternal life. But if today's kids and students don't have the same dots to connect, we need new connection points.

Let's look to the Bible's solution in 1 Corinthians 1:18-25.

> *For the word of the cross is foolishness to those who are perishing, but it is the power of God to us who are being saved. For it is written, "I will destroy the wisdom of the wise, and I will set aside the intelligence of the intelligent."*

> *Where is the one who is wise? Where is the teacher of the law? Where is the debater of this age? Hasn't God made the world's wisdom foolish? For since, in God's wisdom, the world did not know God through wisdom, God was pleased to save those who believe through the foolishness of what is preached. For the Jews ask for signs and the Greeks seek wisdom, but we preach Christ crucified, a stumbling block to the Jews and foolishness to the Gentiles. Yet to those who are called, both Jews and Greeks, Christ is the power of God and the wisdom of God, because God's foolishness is wiser than human wisdom, and God's weakness is stronger than human strength.*

Paul started with the foundation of different cultural narratives and connected each cultural belief to the message of Jesus. He addressed the cultural idolatry of the Greeks (wisdom) and of the Jews (power). He customized his explanation to each, explaining that the cross is the true wisdom to the Greeks and the true power to the Jews. Rather than assuming a shared set of beliefs, Paul connected each unique cultural narrative to the gospel.

Starting with sin and heaven makes sense to someone whose cultural narrative is *"the meaning of life is to be good."* But for kids and students whose cultural narrative is *"the meaning of life is to create your identity,"* we need different dots. We need to identify different starting points that help kids and students connect the felt needs they are experiencing as a result of their secular worldview to the message of Jesus.

Kids and students feel lonely and disconnected because their lives feel like a performance in which as they act out each identity they create for themselves. But Jesus offers the only identity that isn't based on human whims or performance. Jesus offers an identity based on His character and His work on the cross. When we recognize the waters kids and students are swimming in and learn to meet them in the fishbowl, we create opportunities for them to feel heard, understood, and receptive to what we have to share.

A starting point like this lays the foundation for kids and students to be open to hear the gospel. When church becomes a place that understands the culture kids come from, it is more likely to become a place where they feel seen and known, rather than a place they can't wait to leave. Over the course of time they ask their parents to attend more frequently, listen more attentively, and believe more readily.

WE DON'T LIVE IN A MORALISTIC AGE WHERE WE NEED TO PROVE PEOPLE TO BE SINNERS, WE LIVE IN AN ANXIOUS AGE, WHERE WE NEED TO PROVE TO PEOPLE THEY'RE WORTH SOMETHING.

—SAM ALLBERRY

FLIP THE SCRIPT:
FROM "HEAR" TO "HERE"

CHURCH SHOULD BE THE ANSWER TO THE CULTURE CRISIS

SATISFACTION WITH CHURCH IS WANING

NON-CHRISTIANS:

"Church is no longer relevant in today's world."

CHURCHED ADULTS:

"I leave the worship service feeling disappointed by the experience at least half the time."

CHURCHED ADULTS:

"A growing number of people I know are tired of the usual type of church experience."

As believers, we know that Jesus is the answer to both the cultural need for belonging and the cultural question of identity. We want church to be the place people come to encounter Jesus, discovering both belonging and a new identity.

To its credit, the church has recognized its waning impact on society and has tried many strategies to appeal to the lost. Unfortunately, research indicates that those strategies aren't working. "Attractional" church strategies tried to appeal to secular culture but may have over-focused on numerical growth and over-valued entertainment. "Relevant" church strategies concentrated efforts toward looking cool to outsiders but may have over-focused on image and come off as lacking authenticity. "Moral Therapeutic" approaches focused exclusively on the goal of happiness, resulting in tepid cultural Christianity.

Despite these efforts to appeal to outsiders, Americans' confidence in church has dropped to a record low. In 1973, the church was the most highly rated institution in Gallup's Confidence Ratings for Institutions, outranking the military, the U.S. Supreme Court, banks, small businesses, and ten other institutions. In 2022, fewer than 14% of adults said they have "a great deal of confidence" in the church. Confidence within the younger generation is even lower. Only 10% of 18-34 years olds report having a great deal of confidence in the church.[16]

In 2020, Barna looked at Americans' relationship to church. Among non-Christians, 52% agreed that church is no longer relevant in today's world. Among churchgoers, 32% say that they leave the worship service feeling disappointed by the experience at least half the time, and 57% say that a growing number of people they know are tired of the usual type of church experience.[17]

AMERICA'S CONFIDENCE IN THE CHURCH HAS FALLEN STEADILY OVER THE LAST 50 YEARS

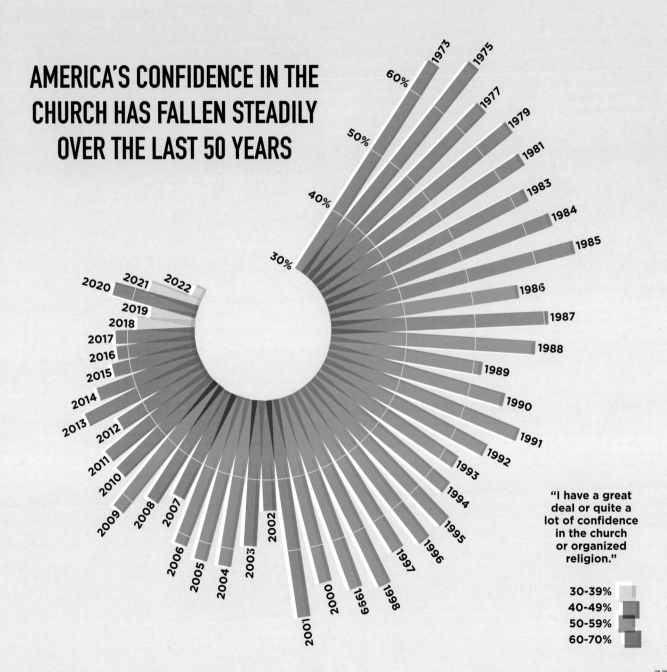

"I have a great deal or quite a lot of confidence in the church or organized religion."

- 30-39%
- 40-49%
- 50-59%
- 60-70%

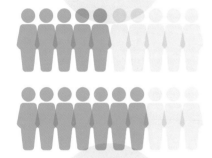

RELEVANCE MATTERS WHEN IT COMES TO YOUNG ADULTS STAYING IN CHURCH

50%
of young adults who left church found sermons to be irrelevant.

68%
of young adults who stayed in church found sermons to be relevant.

Lifeway Research looked at young adults who grew up attending church then dropped out. This study found that among those who stayed in church, 68% said they had found their youth leader's sermons were relevant to their lives. Among those who dropped out of church, only 50% said they had found their youth leader's sermons relevant.[18]

If we consider kids and students growing up in a post-Christian world that has no foundational belief in sin, moral law, eternity, or heaven, is it surprising that they might find the church lacking in relevance? Is it surprising they long for a place where legitimate doubt is permissible or even expected?

WE'VE ASSUMED INACCURATE STARTING POINTS

Let's look through the lens of the fishbowl for a moment and imagine what it might feel like for a kid or student who has never been to church before. She doesn't know any answers. The songs aren't familiar. Her teachers say weird things like "blood of Jesus" and "Habakkuk." She doesn't know the memory verse everyone else has been working on for weeks.

We've approached ministry assuming kids and students have church experience as a starting point. Without meaning to, we've built a culture that quietly says, "You don't belong." If we are going to love like Jesus loves, then we shouldn't expect kids and students to break into this church culture that's alien to them. Instead, we should remove our inaccurate assumptions and meet them where they are.

*Without meaning to,
we've built a culture
that quietly says,
"You don't belong."*

35

WE CAN'T ASSUME THE CHILDREN OF MILLENNIALS AND GEN X HAVE PRIOR CHURCH EXPERIENCE

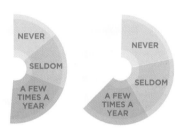

53%
of Generation X attend church a few times a year or less.

64%
of Millennials attend church a few times a year or less.

What other ministry habits reveal that we assume kids and students have prior church experience?

- Talking to them as though they already know what the Bible is, that the Bible is true, and how to find things in it
- Asking knowledge-based Bible questions
- Assuming they already know each other and the teacher
- Expecting them to feel safe and included just by showing up
- Assuming they arrive ready to learn
- Expecting they will trust and believe their teacher
- Reviewing previous weeks' lessons or memory work
- Using "churchy" language
- Assuming they know where to go/what to do in your space

As Lifeway talks to Kids Ministers who are reaching unchurched kids about their top unmet needs in curriculum, we hear answers like "relevant to culture," "works for both churched and unchurched kids," "relevant to unchurched or inner city." These point toward a gap in our ability to talk to kids who lack church experience.[19]

As we saw in chapter 1, modern culture has indoctrinated kids and students to crave freedom and self-definition, to reject external authority, and to believe humans are inherently good. Given that, we may be wrongly assuming they have the dots to connect with what we are teaching. Traditional ministry teaching models look something like this: HEAR—BELIEVE—SHARE. Taking for granted that kids and students can hear the gospel, move to believing in Christ, and begin sharing their faith assumes the dots for understanding the gospel were already there, waiting to be connected. This approach was successful in the past when kids' and students' cultural understanding of how the world works was compatible with Christian truths. This method may still work to some degree in areas of the country less influenced by post-Christian thought. But many of us need to change our starting point.

TRADITIONAL MINISTRY MODEL

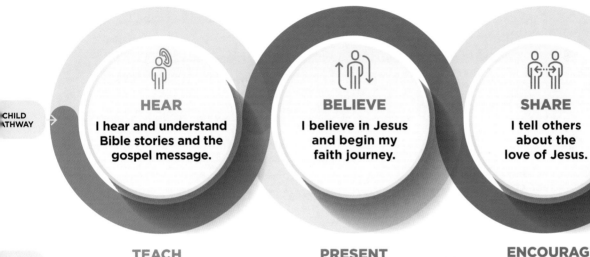

CHILD PATHWAY

HEAR
I hear and understand Bible stories and the gospel message.

BELIEVE
I believe in Jesus and begin my faith journey.

SHARE
I tell others about the love of Jesus.

CHURCH STRATEGY

TEACH
THE BIBLE

Teach the Bible according to a scope and sequence with a wise discipleship plan.

PRESENT
THE GOSPEL

Present the gospel at the end of each lesson or at regular intervals and offer the opportunity to repent and be saved.

ENCOURAGE
EVANGELISM

Remind kids often that they should be telling their friends about the love of Jesus. Hold events like VBS and encourage kids to invite friends.

FLIP THE SCRIPT FROM HEAR TO HERE

We can't assume hearing the gospel will be a sufficient first step in a child's faith journey. We must start from a new place. Rather than defining HEAR as the first step in a child's faith journey, let's flip that HEAR to HERE. We aren't assuming readiness to learn. We aren't assuming prior knowledge. We are assuming only presence—I AM HERE. That's it.

HERE. When we flip the script from beginning with HEAR to beginning with HERE, it changes how we approach a child. Rather than a focus on disseminating information, we become focused on making sure that a child feels welcome, included, and wants to come back. If the church prioritizes breaking down any barriers to belonging as first order, kids and students feel more comfortable, known, wanted, included, and celebrated. This breaks down barriers for them to hear. As ministry leaders, we often feel like *This might be my only opportunity to talk to this child, so I need to make it count.* We need to be careful that doesn't lead us to rush headlong into sharing information before we've earned kids' trust.

LISTENING. When a child feels included and connected, he can engage with others and begin to listen. Strategies for kids and students in the listening stage center around making sure they *stay engaged*. It's vital they keep coming back and listening long enough to begin to understand—kids and students who don't enjoy the experience don't want to return. We need to find ways to create engaging experiences to help them integrate quickly and fast-forward to feeling like a part of the group.

UNDERSTANDING. As a child continues to return and listen, she will understand increasingly more. The best strategy for kids and students in this stage is to teach foundational truths about who God is and what He is like, with no prior knowledge necessary. The strategy for the church is to focus on making every child an insider, treating every session like the first week, and avoiding practices that might alienate newcomers. The goal is to avoid having any child feel dumb or embarrassed by what he does not yet know. Every session should stand alone in terms of value and impact, no matter how often someone attends.

Focusing on belonging and relationships is absolutely critical for kids and students in these first three pre-faith stages. It keeps them returning for more. It allows time to build a relationship and trust between teacher and student. It creates the right conditions for heart transformation.

 BELIEVING. Having set the stage for heart transformation, we're praying that a child's heart will then be prepared to believe in Jesus. Gospel conversations should never just be tacked on to the end of a session. The church should make sure kids and students hear the gospel repeatedly but from a slightly different context each time, according to what else they are learning about, who they are, and who God is.

 GROWING. Having believed in Jesus and begun their faith journeys, we want kids and students to become more like Him and display His character. The church should nurture an identity based in God's character. We want to help kids and students understand they don't need to invent their own identities; their identities are defined by who God is and what He is like.

 REACHING. As a child grows in his relationship with God, he will grow in his desire to go, serve, and tell others about Jesus. The church needs to create opportunities for kids to serve their communities alongside volunteers and parents. Being a welcomed person plants the seed for a child to become someone who welcomes others.

Each child moves through these steps at his own pace, not on our schedule. We expect to have kids and students in every one of these stages every week, so the church should employ all the strategies all the time to meet the needs of kids wherever they are in their spiritual growth.

NEXTGEN MINISTRY MODEL

CHILD PATHWAY →

I AM HERE
I feel welcome here, included, and want to come back.

LISTENING
I am engaging with others, feel connected, and want to listen.

UNDERSTANDING
I understand increasingly more about who God is and what He is like.

CHURCH STRATEGY →

BREAK DOWN
BARRIERS TO BELONGING

Go the extra mile to make sure every single child feels comfortable, known, wanted, included, celebrated, and connected so he can be ready to listen.

ENGAGE
KIDS WITH FUN EXPERIENCES

When kids and students cheer for a team, work together on a relay, or build something together, they integrate quickly and fast-forward to a sense of belonging. Group games foster identity/belonging, and open ears to hear spiritual truths.

LEVEL
THE PLAYING FIELD

Foundational truths about who God is and what He is like—with no prior knowledge necessary—make everyone an insider. Every session should be treated like the first week, avoiding anything that would alienate.

BELIEVING

I believe in Jesus and begin my faith journey.

GROWING

I become more like Jesus, and display His character.

REACHING

I serve my community and tell others about the love of Jesus.

OFFER
THE GOSPEL IN CONTEXT

The weekly gospel conversation should never be arbitrarily tacked on to the end of a session but framed around content kids are studying. Kids should hear the gospel repeatedly but always with an on-ramp from the session.

NURTURE
AN IDENTITY BASED ON GOD'S CHARACTER

Helping kids and students understand that one's identity is defined by who God is and what He is like offers true understanding of identity and belonging.

GIVE
OPPORTUNITIES TO GO, SERVE, AND TELL

Create opportunities for kids and students to serve their community alongside volunteers and parents. Serving with others builds a lifestyle of sharing their faith. Being a welcomed person plants the seed for a child to become someone who welcomes others.

THE CULTURAL NEED FOR BIBLICAL BELONGING AND TRUE IDENTITY

As we've seen, the key emotional need of this generation is to feel known and seen and to experience a sense of belonging. The key question of this generation is "Who Am I?" If we build an environment that meets their key emotional needs and teach content that answers their key cultural questions, we have a better hope of reaching this generation. These two ideas fuse together to form one interconnected approach to ministry. When kids and students feel safe and known by others, they become open to learn about who God is. When they base their identities in who God is, they break free of the cultural pressure to get their identities right. Instead, they discover their identities are already defined by the God who made them. This freedom compels kids and students to want others to know God too.

Strategies for kids and students in the first three stages of the NextGen Model (Here, Listening, Understanding) are more relational—leaning heavily toward building an environment of extravagant welcome and belonging (more about this in chapter 3). Strategies for kids and students in the second three stages (Believing, Growing, Reaching) lean more heavily toward teaching timely content that equips them to follow Jesus in a culture that bombards them with expressive individualism. Kids and students need to learn that their identity is defined by who God is, and that's where they'll find true belonging (more about this in chapter 4).

Traditionally, it made sense to start with content first when kids and students had church experience as a starting point. As the world becomes increasingly secular, we need to do more relational work up front to earn the right to be heard and the trust of our listeners. This allows us to challenge secular cultural beliefs and connect kids' and students' cultural narratives to Jesus. We need to flip the script from a traditional content-first approach to a relationship-first approach.

THE NEW NEXTGEN MINISTRY MODEL MEETS THE CULTURAL NEED FOR BELONGING AND ANSWERS THE CULTURAL QUESTION ABOUT IDENTITY.

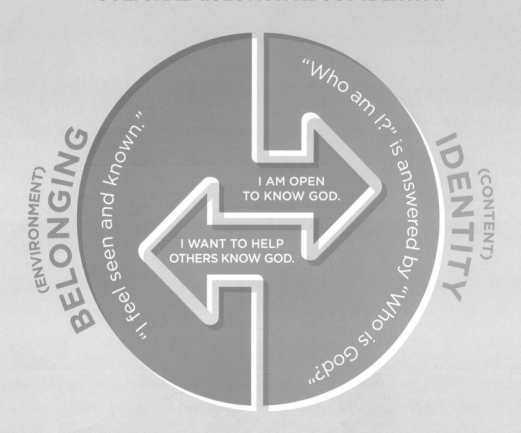

WHEN CHILDREN EXPERIENCE AN ENVIRONMENT OF BELONGING, THEY FEEL SEEN AND KNOWN BY OTHERS AND BECOME OPEN TO LEARN ABOUT WHO GOD IS. WHEN KIDS AND STUDENTS BASE THEIR IDENTITIES IN WHO GOD IS, THEY LOVE GOD AND WANT OTHERS TO KNOW HIM.

FLIP THE SCRIPT:
FROM SEEN TO KNOWN

INTENTIONAL STRATEGIES

In the first two chapters we have seen how students and kids are trending away from the Christian faith and immersing themselves in the cultural philosophy of expressive individualism. In the next few chapters, we will turn our attention to some intentional strategies to help students and kids recognize who they are and where they belong within this cultural landscape.

THE BUZZ OF "BELONGING"

We want kids and students to know that they belong. Generally speaking, *belonging* has a positive connotation in our culture. But in some instances it can be polarizing—especially in the church. Perhaps this stems from the popular saying that you can "belong before you believe." Many churches have used this saying to convey a sense of welcomeness and hospitality for newcomers who may not have a relationship with God. However, there are some who interpret this phrase to mean anyone can be part of the kingdom of God, including those who have not trusted in Jesus for salvation. We define belonging as a place where kids feel welcomed, seen, and known. Belonging does not mean everyone is eligible for church membership or the ordinances. For this book, belonging is about generous friendship. Pursuing a relationship-first approach to ministry involves helping kids and students feel seen and known so that they are open to knowing God.

Belonging is a fundamental human need, right behind food, water, and safety.[20] For children, experiencing a sense of belonging in school has strong, positive effects on both emotion and cognition. Belonging in school is found to improve mental health and emotional well-being, reduce feelings of alienation, and reduce anxiety and depression.[21] Why would we expect belonging to have a different impact at church?

We are driven by five genetic needs: survival, love and belonging, power, freedom, and fun.

—William Glasser

The question is, are we—the church—doing this? Are we creating a sense of belonging when kids and students walk in the door? Are we showing a continued hospitality that engages kids and ensures they not only feel seen but also known? Unfortunately, the answer statistically is no.

WHY ARE WE LOSING GEN Z?

Numerous studies show that churches have not met the relational needs of its younger generations. Sixty-six percent of churched kids stop attending regularly between the ages of 18 and 22. Thirty-two percent of dropouts said they felt judged by adults in their church. Twenty-nine percent of young adults who dropped out said they didn't feel connected to people in the church.[22] When you ask them why they stopped, over half the reasons are because of relationships. Furthermore, adults are missing the true blessing of passing on the faith to students and kids. The numbers are chilling and convicting, pointing to the underlying reason why the next generation is leaving the church.

These statistics seem to show that, while we have said relationships are important to sharing the gospel, we can't afford to merely give lip service to the importance of relationships. Prioritizing relationships within the church is vital. Relationships position students and kids to be able to hear what we have to say.

BUT MY CHURCH IS GREAT AT HOSPITALITY!

Studies show that there is no shortage of creative ways to welcome newcomers.[23] On any given Sunday, there are parking attendants helping new families find a close-up place to park, smiling volunteers with name tags welcoming people at the door, even church staff giving out gifts to show hospitality. Some churches have dedicated staff positions and volunteer teams to focus on first impressions and follow-up. Churches across the

66% OF CHURCHED KIDS STOP ATTENDING CHURCH REGULARLY BETWEEN THE AGES OF 18-22

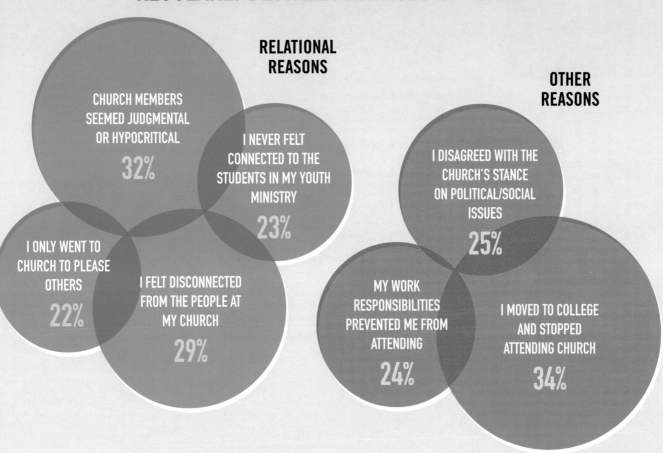

RELATIONAL REASONS

OTHER REASONS

CHURCH MEMBERS SEEMED JUDGMENTAL OR HYPOCRITICAL
32%

I NEVER FELT CONNECTED TO THE STUDENTS IN MY YOUTH MINISTRY
23%

I DISAGREED WITH THE CHURCH'S STANCE ON POLITICAL/SOCIAL ISSUES
25%

I ONLY WENT TO CHURCH TO PLEASE OTHERS
22%

I FELT DISCONNECTED FROM THE PEOPLE AT MY CHURCH
29%

MY WORK RESPONSIBILITIES PREVENTED ME FROM ATTENDING
24%

I MOVED TO COLLEGE AND STOPPED ATTENDING CHURCH
34%

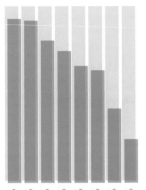

96% Opportunity to meet the pastor after service
95% Greeters at the entrances
83% Cards guests are asked to complete
78% Central location where guests can learn about the church
69% Time during service to personally welcome guests
65% Information session about the church
42% Gifts for guests
24% Greeters in the parking lot

country have adopted engaging practices to welcome others into their space. Rarely do you visit a church where there is not someone to lead you to the right place, introduce your family to the children's leader, or help you find a great seat in the worship service.[24]

Churches are also usually strategic with follow-up—sending postcards, making phone calls, even texting a word of encouragement to newcomers. We make sure that people know who we are, what to do, and when to come back. They can hardly escape being seen when they walk in the door.

However, helping people feel seen is not enough. For the most part, we are stopping short at going to the next step of helping people feel known, which comes from deeper connections and relationships. Friendly faces are a good start, but when people are not connected, they don't want to return—especially our kids and students. Many newcomers to our churches are disengaging because of a lack of authentic relationship. They feel judged, disconnected, or they are trying to please others.

How, then, do we create the kind of culture that makes our students and kids not only want to walk in the door but also excited to return again and again?

EXTRAVAGANT WELCOME AND RADICAL HOSPITALITY

It's time for us to reevaluate our approach. We don't need another welcome team. Instead, we need to engage newcomers in relationships, to connect with them and help them feel known so we can introduce them to Jesus. Non-religious people often crave Christian community long before they crave Christian faith. This type of hospitality doesn't live within a team, but within a whole church culture of engagement and intentionality.

We need collectively to live our faith openly and publicly in our communities so that when kids and students who don't know God see His presence in our lives, they will be drawn to know Him themselves and honor Him (1 Peter 2:12). When we provide a place for kids to experience the extravagant welcome of Jesus through the radical hospitality of His people, we prepare their hearts to hear and respond to the gospel.

Radical hospitality and extravagant welcome are personal. They look people in the eye and call them by name. They connect the disconnected into relationships. They let people know they are seen, known, and valued here. They avoid using language that makes newcomers feel excluded or confused. They go the extra mile to create a culture that's comfortable, accepting, and approachable to everyone who walks through the door. They create a compelling context of biblical belonging that connects the disconnected in a Christ-centered community for the purpose of inciting a transformational encounter with Jesus.

None of these things happen by accident. We must intentionally go out of our way to engage kids, students, and their families in ways that are meaningful and authentic so we can introduce them to God.

EXPECT KIDS IN THE FIRST THREE STAGES

Look back at the pathway shown in chapter 2 on pages 40-41. Notice the first three steps—Here, Listening, Understanding—are pre-faith steps. Traditional ministry models often start with a content-first step of believing. But as we've already uncovered, many kids and students of this generation have a different starting point. They don't think in the same ways or hold to the same values as many of the adults they encounter at church. When we assume nothing but the fact that a child is present, the number one goal should be making him feel like he belongs, providing emotional safety and meeting his psychological need to be known. This all begins in step one when a kid walks in your space for the first time.

Creating a culture of belonging motivates us to be intentional about how we move a child toward an openness of listening, understanding, and believing. When you bombard a kid with information before he is ready to hear, you may alienate him further. When you try to "sell" a student on a new belief system before you've shown you care, he may sense manipulation. When a child or student walks into your space for the first few times, she probably feels like an outsider. Our goal should be to help students and kids see themselves as insiders who feel comfortable to not only participate but also contribute to the group knowing they are in a place where they belong.

FROM OUTSIDERS TO INSIDE CONTRIBUTORS

We have assumed kids and students arrive at church comfortable and ready to greet friends and learn. Today, many of theses kids and students are either first-time attendees or (even more likely) infrequent attendees who may arrive feeling like outsiders.

Kids who feel like outsiders experience fear and insecurity and don't learn effectively. As kids increasingly assimilate into the group, their fear of being embarrassed or marginalized decreases and their ability to learn and contribute increases. We aim to intentionally design the church experience to move each child toward feeling like an insider and contributing to the group. It's important to visualize the experience newcomers have, being mindful to design the content and flow of a church experience to address each phase they might go through in the duration of a typical one-hour session.

The model on the following pages show each phase from the Outsider–In methodology. This diagram represents how to design an experience that strategically moves kids and students

ACT WISELY
TOWARD
OUTSIDERS,
MAKING THE
MOST OF
THE TIME.

—COLOSSIANS 4:5

to a level of comfort when they arrive so that by the end of the hour they feel confident enough to participate fully. When we strategically implement radical hospitality, we help a child move from fear and anxiety to belonging and safety.

When kids and students arrive at church and feel celebrated and known by leaders and other peers, they feel psychologically safe to engage and participate. As we engage them in games and activities that are built around relationships, they begin to feel included in the group. With our actions we are saying, "You belong here. You are part of this team." As they assimilate into finding a place on the team, they further join in participation.

As kids and students reach the point of participation, they feel more comfortable within the group to be ready to listen and learn about God and the Bible. Then they become more like insiders, engaging in questions and applying what they learn. This Outsider–In methodology helps position leaders to meet children where they are in the first three stages of the NextGen Ministry model and create an environment of deeper engagement, understanding, and relational trust.

Notice the value of relationships in this model. We can't expect kids and students to move toward inside contributors without the relational trust we build as leaders. Start building relational trust from the moment kids walk in. Begin by showing extravagant welcome, celebrating them, getting to know them as people. This helps them move toward the valuable moments where they fully learn, contribute, and apply the biblical content they are learning.

We must make relationship-first ministry strategies a priority. Kids and students aren't going to care what we know until they know that we care. They are less likely to have open hearts to hear the message of the gospel if they don't feel like they belong. It's easy for people to walk away from a program, but it's much harder to walk away from rich relationships.

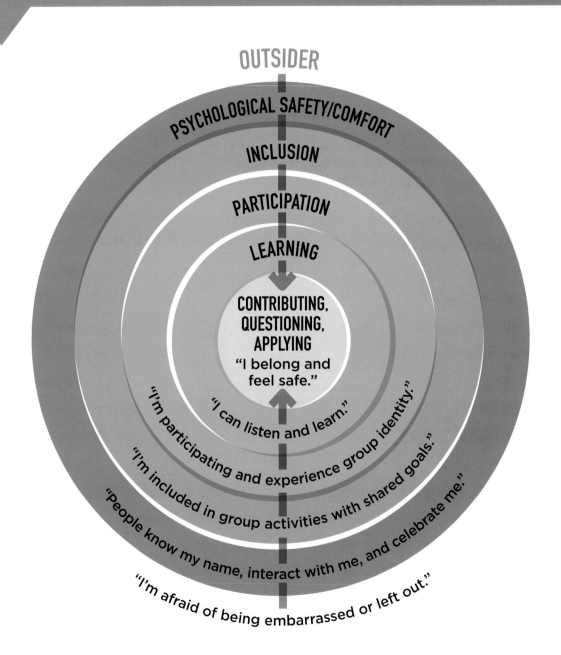

OUTSIDER

PSYCHOLOGICAL SAFETY/COMFORT

INCLUSION

PARTICIPATION

LEARNING

CONTRIBUTING,
QUESTIONING,
APPLYING
"I belong and
feel safe."

"I can listen and learn."

"I'm participating and experience group identity."

"I'm included in group activities with shared goals."

"People know my name, interact with me, and celebrate me."

"I'm afraid of being embarrassed or left out."

PSYCHOLOGICAL SAFETY/COMFORT—The Child/Student Experiences:
"People know my name, interact with me, and celebrate me."
Our Response: Structure arrival time around making kids feel celebrated and known by their group leader and known by other kids. Examples might include playing open-entry games, doing get-to-know-you activities, and greeting each kid with an extreme welcome!

INCLUSION—The Child/Student Experiences: *"I'm included in group activities with shared goals."* **Our Response:** Playing group games and activities around a shared goal helps kids feel included—even needed on a team or small group.

OUTSIDER—
The Child/Student Experiences:
"I'm afraid of being embarrassed or left out."
Our Response: Whether a visitor, an infrequent attendee, or someone who normally attends at a different time, many kids arrive feeling like an outsider. It's critical to move them toward psychological safety and comfort as quickly as possible.

PARTICIPATION—The Child/Student Experiences:
"I'm participating and experiencing group identity."
Our Response: Consider incorporating lighthearted competition between small groups. Cheering for their team helps kids identify as a part of their group and further assimilate. The "I" begins to feel like "we" during this stage.

LEARNING—The Child/Student Experiences: *"I can listen and learn."* **Our Response:** By this point in the session, kids feel emotionally comfortable in their groups and are emotionally ready to listen and learn. Tell the Bible story knowing you may be talking to someone who has never heard of God or the Bible.

CONTRIBUTING, QUESTIONING, APPLYING—The Child/Student Experiences: *"I belong and feel safe to contribute and question without fear of being embarrassed or marginalized."* **Our Response:** Reinforce Bible content by providing opportunities for kids to ask questions and enjoy sharing from their hearts.

WHEN YOU LOOK AT CHILDHOOD PREDICTORS OF SPIRITUAL HEALTH IN YOUNG ADULTS, SEVERAL ARE RELATIONAL

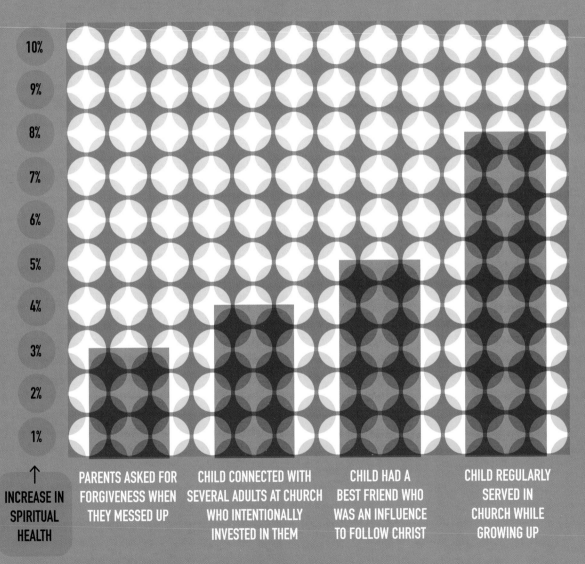

10%
9%
8%
7%
6%
5%
4%
3%
2%
1%

↑
INCREASE IN SPIRITUAL HEALTH

PARENTS ASKED FOR FORGIVENESS WHEN THEY MESSED UP

CHILD CONNECTED WITH SEVERAL ADULTS AT CHURCH WHO INTENTIONALLY INVESTED IN THEM

CHILD HAD A BEST FRIEND WHO WAS AN INFLUENCE TO FOLLOW CHRIST

CHILD REGULARLY SERVED IN CHURCH WHILE GROWING UP

FLIP RELATIONSHIPS:
KIDS AND STUDENTS NEED FRIENDS

Kids need four types of relationships to truly connect to the church and experience belonging there. Those relationships can be identified by the acronym FLIP.

F IS FOR FRIENDS

One of the best things we can do to encourage belonging is to help kids and students develop lasting friendships with their peers. Every kid needs to find friends at church. Friendships connect us in belonging. We naturally want to belong and be where our friends are.

F FRIENDS
L LEADERS
I INFLUENCERS
P PASTORS

In the Lifeway Research study *Nothing Less*, children and students who had a best friend who influenced them to follow Christ while growing up had a higher score of spiritual maturity as adults.[25] This means that they did not leave the church, beating the statistics that suggest that a majority of students do leave the church while in college, many never to return. Instead, the study says those who found friends in the church as kids are more likely to thrive in their faith as adults.

As ministry leaders, we actively need to design experiences that are specifically intended to help kids and students find, form, and foster friendships. When kids are expected to sit still and face forward quietly without interacting, they are not able to form these important friendships. Informed leaders create intentional times to fuel friendships. Kids and students who have a friend, or multiple friends, at church are more likely to attend with greater frequency and regularity than those who do not.

The following ideas are just a few ways to reframe thinking about how to approach fostering friendships in your ministry. As a result, the meaningful relationships at church could point kids and students to a lifetime of lasting faith.

A DAY WITHOUT
A FRIEND IS LIKE
A POT WITHOUT A
SINGLE DROP OF
HONEY LEFT INSIDE.

—WINNIE THE POOH

1. **Watch for ways to connect kids and students with one another:** As a ministry leader, you have a unique opportunity to help kids and students make connections. You know names, who goes to what school, and maybe even individual interests such as favorite sports and hobbies. With this information, you can be sure that students and kids find some common interests with one another—and talk about those things!

2. **Notice the introverts:** Some kids don't naturally gravitate to socializing with others and may need help making friends. Notice and involve introverts in appropriate ways, realizing that the relational needs for introverts and extroverts are different. Make it your goal for each child to have at least one friend at church.

3. **Evaluate your programming:** Does the church experience you are providing foster relationships or is your programming creating barriers to developing relationships? While they may be hard questions, we need to regularly evaluate our spaces and programs for roadblocks that might lead a child to feel alienated or marginalized. Changing the focus to a relational emphasis vs. instructional guidance may be the key to unlocking a world of potential friendships.

4. **Assume every meeting is full of kids and students who feel like outsiders:** Look for intentional ways to connect them to each other and to leaders. It is no longer adequate to simply assume that every child wants to be there or that any child has previous biblical knowledge. By changing our mindset, we will be better able to look for intentional ways to connect kids and students to each other and to leaders.

5. **Plan intentional relationship-building time:** Group games are a great way to do this. When students cheer for their team, run a relay, or solve a problem together, it fast-forwards them into a sense of inclusion and belonging.

Church should be a place where friends are found! Create the culture that fosters friendships and watch the kids and students in your ministry thrive.

RELATIONAL EVANGELISM AND RADICAL HOSPITALITY

Our communities are filled with lonely people who long for authentic connection through caring friendships. Engaging a culture that does not know God, trust the church, or believe the Bible requires us to take the message of the gospel outside the walls of our buildings. In a post-Christian culture, effective evangelism is relational. Fewer and fewer unchurched, under-churched, and de-churched people are willing to accept cold invitations from strangers to visit unknown churches We need to enter into our neighbors' lives and welcome them into ours. Once we know our neighbors, we can bring them into our church communities and introduce them to Jesus. The church must actively go out, seek out, search out, and build up connections with our unbelieving neighbors.

Consider how your church can engage with neighbors in driveways and around backyard firepits. This may mean evaluating the church calendar to make strategic decisions to have people in neighborhoods more than on church campuses. Help those in your circles recognize the opportunities they have at parks, at soccer games, and by taco trucks. We must seek to actively reach our non-believing neighbors by building relational bridges that allow us to lead them to Christ in a context of true and caring friendship. Our non-Christian friends need to know that an invitation to church is not based on a religious agenda but is an extension of genuine friendship.

This kind of radical hospitality doesn't passively wait; it actively watches. Guide leaders to notice newcomers and speak value over them. Let's make our churches places where people who don't yet know God can learn about Him in a warm and welcoming environment that connects them with committed believers who show them Jesus. We can better reach our neighbors by creating a church culture that is oriented toward receiving and welcoming the uninitiated and goes to radical lengths to connect them into our biblical communities of faith before they come to belief.

The influence of one loving leader can be immeasurably beneficial in the faith journey of a child.

FLIP RELATIONSHIPS:
KIDS AND STUDENTS NEED LEADERS

 IS FOR LEADERS

All children need to have adult leaders who care about them and know their names, their needs, and their situations. Kids and students need to know there is a leader who misses them when they're not there and celebrates them when they are. The influence of one leader can be incredibly powerful in the life of a child. Research indicates that children who feels connected to several adults at church while growing up is more likely to become spiritually healthy young adults. (See page 56.)[26] Content is more readily accepted when children trust and respect their leader. Trust and respect must be earned over time by a leader who genuinely cares. The influence of one loving leader can be immeasurably beneficial in the faith journey of a child. .

FLIP RELATIONSHIPS:
KIDS AND STUDENTS NEED INFLUENCERS

 IS FOR INFLUENCERS

While kids need to have one adult leader who knows and cares about them personally, they also need the influence of a broader faith community in the church. Children need to see other invested adults and older kids who are involved in the church, committed to their faith, and connected in relationships within the church. These may be other group leaders, game and recreation leaders, greeters, stage hosts, worship leaders, parents of their friends, or older kids. The influence of older kids and young adults can be especially impactful, as younger children may aspire to be like them. When kids see these influencers throughout the church loving Jesus and living for God, they will be drawn to do so themselves.

THE ONLY CAPITAL BETWEEN TEACHER AND STUDENT IN THE TWENTY-FIRST CENTURY IS THE DEPTH OF THE RELATIONSHIP THAT IS ESTABLISHED.

—TIM ELMORE

If I could relive my
life, I would devote
my entire ministry
to reaching
children for God.

—Dwight L. Moody

FLIP RELATIONSHIPS: KIDS AND STUDENTS NEED PASTORS

 IS FOR PASTORS

Kids and students need to know that the pastor, or pastors, of the church are more than personas on a platform. They need to know that the pastor of the church is their pastor too. We, kids and student leaders, need to welcome and invite pastors to enter into the kids and student areas. Pastors need to know and be known, see and be seen, and hear and be heard in the kids and student ministry areas. It is important for kids to have a personal connection with pastors and for pastors to be personally invested in what's happening in kids and student ministry areas.

Invite your pastor to share a devotion or a word of encouragement to kids or students during a group time or to speak one night at camp. Encourage pastors to walk through the kids ministry hallway and high-five the volunteers and kids. They can sit down for 10 minutes and make a craft at a preschool table. That 10-minute investment allows kids to see a friend up front in a worship service as a friend rather than as a stranger.

DISCIPLESHIP IN RELATIONSHIP

These relationships—friends, leaders, influencers, and pastors—help kids in their discipleship journey. Discipleship happens in the context of relationship. It assumes a "walking together" wherein the disciple is led, taught, and apprenticed by someone who instructs and invests in him on a personal level.

Making disciples is more than teaching. It is more than an assent to a philosophy. Making disciples is about more than service. It is more than social connection. Disciples are followers. Disciples are apprentices. Disciples are imitators.

Discipleship includes two key aspects:

- **Walking together.** This is the context; one that requires a personal relationship with a trusted, respected, and influential leader.
- **Talking together.** This is the content; the transference of spiritual truth, instruction, wisdom, and application.

Deuteronomy 6:4-7 frames these aspects of discipleship in the context of the family:

> *"Listen, Israel, The Lord our God. The Lord is one. Love the Lord your God with all your heart, with all your soul, and with all your strength. These words that I am giving you today are to be in your heart. Repeat them to your children. **Talk about them when you sit in your house and when you walk along the road, when you lie down and when you get up."*** *(Emphasis added.)*

Theses verses describe the training up of children in the faith as a process of talking together while walking together so that children become like their parents.

Likewise, Jesus modeled this relational side-by-side discipleship model in the New Testament. Discipleship, for Jesus' close followers, was a beautiful blend of walking with, talking with, and becoming like Jesus. If we are going to make disciples who imitate the ways, works, and words of Jesus, we also need to imitate how Jesus developed relationships with His followers.

For more than 100 years, traditional Western ministry has largely been conducted in classroom settings that look and feel much like the school environments where students are taught science, math, or history. Even the term "Sunday School" hints at the educational foundation that underlies the predominant approach to ministry.

*Making disciples is
more than teaching ...
Disciples are followers.
Disciples are apprentices.
Disciples are imitators.*

God has used the traditional Sunday School model to His glory for many years, and it is still an effective approach in many contexts. However, the best Sunday School teachers are arguably not those who teach with the most authority, accuracy, or oratory excellence, but rather those who take a personal interest in the children or students they teach.

This is demonstrated time and again by spiritually mature adults whose testimonies include the names of Sunday School teachers who noticed them, coached them, and cared about them when they were children. Few, if any, can remember the details of even a single lesson. But they will never forget the influence of the leaders who took personal interest in them.

IMITATE ME,

AS I ALSO

IMITATE CHRIST.

—1 CORINTHIANS 11:1

As church leaders, we have a unique opportunity, if not an obligation, to partner with families and volunteers in the spiritual formation and development of kids and students through ministry relationships. We can increase our ministry impact by equipping our families and volunteers with skills that will enable them to cultivate influential relational connections with the kids and students in their circles of influence more effectively.

SCRIPT YOUR FLIP

Implementing ministry strategies that lead with relationships before content does not happen by accident. The flip will always be intentional, not accidental. We must script (plan) our flip (strategy).

When we prioritize the fostering of relationships, we upend the traditional method of ministry that begins with lessons and studies. What we teach is extremely important, and we don't want to minimize this aspect. When we emphasize connection in discipleship relationships, the inputs and outputs are both impacted. Content that is conveyed in a context of trust and respect always yields greater influence.

When we take on the model of relationship-first discipleship, we model the development of relationships that Jesus demonstrated with His followers and help kids and students recognize their true identities in Christ. We guide leaders and learners to walk and talk together so they can discuss real issues of real life in real time. We guide them to observe together what's happening in the world and apply the wisdom of God's Word to their lives.

This is not a short-term strategy. This is a long-term movement. This flip the script methodology of leading with relationships is not some new idea or the current trend. It's going back to the way Jesus did ministry, where He approached ones who were far and invited them to follow Him. Then He walked with them and talked with them, teaching them to love the Lord their God with all their hearts and all their soul and all their strength.

This is discipleship. The church doesn't need a new model for education. The church needs the original model for making disciples.

Trust
+ Respect
—
= Influence

FLIP THE SCRIPT:
FROM IDENTITY LOST TO IDENTITY FOUND IN CHRIST

A CRISIS OF IDENTITY

People long to know who they are, why they exist, and the meaning of their lives. They have a deep desire for purpose, but they are missing their true meaning because real meaning for humans can only be found in relationship with God. A humanity that was made in His image and likeness has lost its connection to the Creator and therefore has lost its frame of reference for understanding its identity. People who don't know God, or aren't willing to look to Him, search constantly for substitute identities in an attempt to fill the void they feel. These identities are often centered on self.

Very few people know that God has something to say about their identity, much less what He has said about who they are.

The voice of the secular world is both pervasive and persuasive. The world inundates kids with messages telling them who they should be or that they can/must choose an identity for themselves. For most kids and students, the voice of Truth is missing entirely as they ponder their identities. This is the case for kids and students both inside and outside the church. Many kids and students from Christian families wrestle to reconcile the onslaught of post-Christian messages anchored in the expressive individualism they hear all week (at school, from friends, online, on TV, and on social media) with the messages they hear at church on Sundays. Often, kids and students translate the messages they hear at church to equate Christianity with Bible knowledge (what I know) and right/wrong behavior (what I do/don't do) rather than identity (who I am). Ultimately, they need to know that knowledge and behavior are empty outside of identity and that discovering their true identities is where the Christian life really begins.

Once you've flipped the script on offering students and kids a full pathway to creating extreme hospitality that leads to relationships, the dynamic changes. Their eyes, ears, hearts, and minds will be open to hear, understand, and believe the truth of the gospel. Biblical content replaces the secular idea that "I need to define myself from within" with the biblical understanding of identity. I am who I am because of who God is.

To counter the attack on identity that we see in our culture, we must have conversations in our churches to help kids discover that one's true identity has already been defined by God. As Tim Keller said, "Identity is received, not achieved."[27] We are made in His image. We bear His likeness. We are the *Imago Dei*. We are defined by God. Our true identity can only be realized when we find it in God through Jesus.

The Lifeway Kids and Lifeway Student teams have worked to identify twelve key identity truths that all kids and students should know about who they are because of who God is.

12 TRUTHS

The 12 truths break down into three categories—God's passion for me, my position before God, and God's purpose for my life—each of which contains four truths about our identity in relation to God's identity revealed in the Bible.

God's PASSION for Me

God has demonstrated a great passion for people from creation to salvation. It is seen in how people were created in His image and likeness as the pinnacle of His "very good" creation. It is supported by the promises that God makes throughout Scripture to be *with* His people and *for* His people. And, it is cemented in the expression of His great love and deep compassion for people through the gift of His Son. God's passion is for all people collectively, but what's more incredible is that His passion is personal for everyone individually. True identity is anchored in the knowledge that God uniquely designed me, knows me, will never leave me, and loves me. Identity is framed, first and foremost, by God's great passion for us.

My POSITION Before God

A person's position before God is a bad news/good news scenario. Although we were all designed in His image, Scripture teaches that God is holy, perfect, and sinless; and we are not. In our natural condition, we are legally guilty of sin that condemns us. We are broken people living in a broken world. The good news is that the condition of our position is changeable, not permanent. We are broken but not beyond repair. Jesus took the punishment that we deserve on Himself. He died and rose again so that we can receive the complete forgiveness that God offers to us through faith in Jesus. Students and kids need to know that in Christ they are made new, declared innocent, and His holiness is reassigned to them. When we are examined by God and found to be "in Christ," we are given a new life, a new start, and a new identity. Without the forgiveness that comes through Jesus, we are broken and separated from God, but in Christ, our identity is made new. In Him we are forgiven, set apart, and kept safe. Our identity is affected by our position before God.

God's PLAN for My Life

God has designed you on purpose and for a purpose. Your life was never meant to be lived in isolation. God's plan is for us to be in relationship with Him and part of a community of believers. We are not meant to worship an unknown and unknowable God. God has revealed who He is through His Word so that we can know Him personally. Just as He knows us and loves us, He wants us to know and love Him. Likewise, God has created us to belong to a community of believers who care for, help, and encourage each other. Our reason for living is only fully realized when we discover and live out God's purpose for our lives. Our identity is realized in His plans for our lives: we are made for community, meant to know God, designed to do good, and here to share Jesus. True identity is driven by God's plan for our lives.

Let's take a closer look at each of the 12 truths.

12 BIBLICAL TRUTHS TO COUNTER CULTURAL ATTACKS ON IDENTITY

GOD'S PASSION FOR ME

I AM KNOWN

I AM UNIQUELY DESIGNED

I AM NEVER ALONE

I AM LOVED

MY POSITION BEFORE GOD

I AM BROKEN

I AM FORGIVEN

I AM SECURE

I AM SET APART

GOD'S PLAN FOR MY LIFE

I AM MADE FOR COMMUNITY

I AM MEANT TO KNOW GOD

I AM DESIGNED FOR A PURPOSE

I AM HERE TO SHARE JESUS

GOD'S PASSION FOR ME

TRUTH #1—
I AM KNOWN

God knows you.

In a culture where kids and students feel invisible and overlooked, they need to know that every part of them is known by the God who made them. Nothing and no one is hidden from Him. There are no secrets that can be kept from Him. Hebrews 4:13 says that nothing in all of creation can hide from God. There is no place kids and students can go that He cannot see them. He knows their thoughts, their motives, and their intentions.

And here is the best part.

Even though God knows everything about us—all of our secrets, the lies, the sins, and the mistakes—He still loves us. Kids may feel like no one notices them, sees them, hears them, or maybe even that no one loves them. Students often feel invisible to those around them, but they are seen and known by God. In fact, they are never out of His sight. God hears every worry, every fear, and every insecurity, and He cares about all of it.

By pointing students and kids to the true identity of who God is, we help them realize their true identities—known and extremely valuable.

You are known by God.

PSALM 139:1-2

Lord, you have searched me and known me. You know when I sit down and when I stand up; you understand my thoughts from far away.

HEBREWS 4:13a

No creature is hidden from him.

1 CORINTHIANS 8:3

But if anyone loves God, he is known by him.

2

COLOSSIANS 1:16

Everything was created by him, in heaven and on earth, the visible and the invisible, whether thrones or dominions or rulers or authorities—all things have been created through him and for him.

REVELATION 4:11

Our Lord and God, you are worthy to receive glory and honor and power, because you have created all things, and by your will they exist and were created.

PSALM 139:13-14

For it was you who created my inward parts; you knit me together in my mother's womb. I will praise you because I have been remarkably and wondrously made. Your works are wondrous, and I know this very well.

TRUTH #2—
I AM UNIQUELY DESIGNED

God designed you.

The Bible tells us that God made everything (Colossians 1:16)—everything in heaven and on earth, the visible and the invisible. All things were made by Him and for Him.

Think about the weight of that truth—the ultimate Designer; the wise Creator; the Master Maker of the galaxies, the God who imagined oceans—He designed every student and kid who comes into your mind right now.

The Bible teaches that God, the ultimate Designer, is intentional (Revelation 4:11). He is wise and purposeful (Psalm 104:24). Nothing exists outside of His control, His plans, or His ultimate purposes (Colossians 1:16).

Why does this matter? Because every detail about the kids and students you teach was determined by God and crafted by His hand. Their height, eye color, the width of their shoulders, the color of their skin, the texture of their hair, the size of their feet, their smiles, the way they think, their voices, the talents they have, their gender—no child is accidental. They were made on purpose and for a purpose.

Voices in culture may tell our kids that they are random, a product of chance, or even a mistake, but God says differently. God says they are unique, wonderful, special creations because they are designed by Him. He made all people who they are and how they are. God does not make mistakes. He makes masterpieces (Ephesians 2:10).

You are designed by God.

TRUTH #3—
I AM NEVER ALONE

3

God is always with you.

At a time when kids and students feel like they are all alone, distant, or in isolation from others, they need to know the identity of the One true God—the One who will never abandon them. The writer of Psalm 139 asked:

"Where can I go to escape your Spirit? Where can I flee from your presence? If I go up to heaven, you are there; if I make my bed in Sheol, you are there. If I fly on the wings of the dawn and settle down on the western horizon, even there your hand will lead me; your right hand will hold on to me. If I say, 'Surely the darkness will hide me, and the light around me will be night'—even the darkness is not dark to you. The night shines like the day; darkness and light are alike to you." (Psalm 139:7-12)

God promises to always be with us no matter what happens because that is who He is. He is the God of fierce loyalty. When we walk through dark valleys, God is there. When we face the unknown, God is there. When we try to run, hide, rebel, and fight against Him, God is still there. His steadfast faithfulness never diminishes, no matter what. He is always faithful, and He is ever-present.

We see the identity of this promise reflected in the identity of Jesus. The prophet Isaiah foretold of the coming Messiah who would be called Immanuel (Isaiah 7:14). Immanuel—God with us—came to make a way for us to be with God forever.

God is not distant. He is near. He sees, He hears, and He loves.

You are never alone.

DEUTERONOMY 31:8

The LORD is the one who will go before you. He will be with you; he will not leave you or abandon you. Do not be afraid or discouraged.

ISAIAH 41:10

Do not fear, for I am with you; do not be afraid, for I am your God. I will strengthen you; I will help you; I will hold on to you with my righteous right hand.

PSALM 23:4a

Even when I go through the darkest valley, I fear no danger, for you are with me.

TRUTH #4—
I AM LOVED

God loves you.

God designed kids and students to be exactly who they are, and He loves them just as they are. In a world where love is conditional, kids and students need to know that God's love is unconditional. The Bible describes God's love as deep, wide, long, and vast (Ephesians 3:18). Unlike other relationships, God's love is not based on what they do, but on who they are—His special creation.

Love isn't just something that God does, it's who He is. God is love (1 John 4:8). God gives His love freely and generously. Like our identity, God's love is something that is received, not achieved.

God did not wait for us to love Him. In fact, the very opposite is true. "But God proves his own love for us in that while we were still sinners, Christ died for us." (Romans 5:8) It was because of the great love with which He loved us, even when we were dead in our sin, that God made a way to make us alive together with Christ. Ephesians 1:5 tells us that He has adopted us as sons and daughters.

God is good. He is steadfast and unchanging. He is faithful, trustworthy, and loving.

You are loved by God.

EPHESIANS 2:4-5

But God, who is rich in mercy, because of his great love that he had for us, made us alive with Christ even though we were dead in trespasses.

1 JOHN 3:1a

See what great love the Father has given us that we should be called God's children—and we are!

JOHN 15:12

This is my command: Love one another as I have loved you.

In a world where love is conditional, kids and students need to know that God's love is unconditional.

TRUTHS 5-8

MY POSITION BEFORE GOD

TRUTH #5—
I AM BROKEN

You are broken.

The reality of this truth hits deeply, and it should. We saw in chapter 1 that most kids and students in this generation do not believe in absolutes. The notions that people are sinful by nature and deserve sin's punishment are antithetical to their worldview. However, this generation is very aware of brokenness. We see the brokenness in our world and in our lives. Our thoughts are broken, our relationships are broken, our motives are broken, and our perceptions are broken.

We can help students recognize that without Jesus, everyone has a positional identity of brokenness before God. When Adam and Eve chose to disobey God, they broke their relationship with Him. Sin is not just the wrong things we do. Sin is woven into our very nature. We are sinners from birth. As we teach kids, we must communicate that the natural default condition of our lives is brokenness.

Fortunately, we are not broken beyond repair, and kids and students need to know where to look to find repair for this brokenness. It is not within. It is not through defining your own identity or trying again and again to reinvent or redefine yourself. This only leads to anxiety, futility, and hopelessness. The answer to brokenness can only come from above. We cannot change our identity of brokenness, but God can. He made a way for us to be fully forgiven. The good news of the gospel begins with bad news.

You are broken.

ISAIAH 53:6

We all went astray like sheep; we all have turned to our own way; and the LORD has punished him for the iniquity of us all.

ROMANS 5:12

Therefore, just as sin entered the world through one man, and death through sin, in this way death spread to all people, because all sinned.

1 JOHN 1:8

If we say, "We have no sin," we are deceiving ourselves, and the truth is not in us.

6

PSALM 86:5

For you, Lord, are kind and ready to forgive, abounding in faithful love to all who call on you.

ROMANS 8:1-2

Therefore, there is now no condemnation for those in Christ Jesus, because the law of the Spirit of life in Christ Jesus has set you free from the law of sin and death.

1 JOHN 1:9

If we confess our sins, he is faithful and righteous to forgive us our sins and to cleanse us from all unrighteousness.

TRUTH #6—
I AM FORGIVEN

God provided forgiveness for you.

Although we are all broken by sin, God does not leave us in our brokenness. God is good and just to judge the evil in our world, beginning with us, and He is merciful to provide forgiveness for our rebellion.

In His mercy and kindness toward us, God provided a solution to our sin problem. Rather than automatically punishing people for their sins, He made a way to reconcile us to Himself by placing our punishment on His perfect Son. Jesus stood in our place. He took our punishment, died on the cross, and rose again so that we can receive a new identity— completely forgiven.

God alone has the power and authority to change our identities. It isn't something we can earn or achieve. It can only be received. This change only comes through faith in Jesus. Second Corinthians 5:21 tells us that God made Jesus (the One who never sinned) to be sin for us, so that in Him we could be forgiven and free.

When we teach about forgiveness in Jesus, we can communicate new identity in a way kids and students understand. God removes our identity of brokenness and gives us an identity of forgiven son or daughter. In Him we are set free from the law of sin and death.

When you put your trust in Jesus, you are completely forgiven.

TRUTH #7—
I AM SET APART

Because of God, you are different now.

How does following Jesus change someone's position before God? As leaders, we can champion the truth that when we belong to God because we have trusted in Jesus, we are set apart. To a student who wants to fit into the culture, to swim in the fishbowl, it is essential to understand that this new identity in Christ is costly. But, disciples of Jesus are not just called to be set apart *from* something. They are called to be set apart *to* Someone.

We can help kids recognize that to be set apart means that each person is a special possession with a special purpose. The biblical word for set apart is *holy*. Something that is holy is "dedicated; something sacred." Holy things are reserved for special uses. This is part of true identity in Jesus.

Being set apart means living in ways that glorify God instead of being shaped by the patterns of behavior of the broken world that doesn't know or acknowledge Him. It means choosing to live life shaped by the words, ways, and actions of Jesus.

We are set apart from our old self-centered lives for new lives in Christ. When you are found in Christ, you receive the true identity that God has prepared for you!

You are special. You are valuable. You are set apart.

DEUTERONOMY 7:6a

For you are a holy people belonging to the LORD your God.

COLOSSIANS 3:1-2

So if you have been raised with Christ, seek the things above, where Christ is, seated at the right hand of God. Set your minds on things above, not on earthly things.

1 PETER 2:9

But you are a chosen race, a royal priesthood, a holy nation, a people for his possession, so that you may proclaim the praises of the one who called you out of darkness into his marvelous light.

8

I AM SECURE

God is steadfast and trustworthy, even in danger.

One of God's great promises is to hold us fast even in times of danger or uncertainty. He is with us in times of disaster. He is our shelter and our safe place. He can be trusted when the reality of our situation is crumbling around us.

This generation is bombarded with content about how unsafe their world is, and with good reason. Terrorism, racial unrest, recession, global competition, complexity, uncertainty—these are just a few of the realities that shape the lives of students and children in our ministries. They do not know a world where these dangers don't exist.

Their world is broken, unsafe, and scary. And, they need to know where they can turn in the midst of frightening circumstances. They need to know the true identity of the God they follow. He is trustworthy. He is steadfast. He is enough. He holds them secure even when their world is uncertain.

Because God is omnipresent, He is always with us. Because He is all-knowing (omniscient), He is always aware of our situations. Psalm 111:7 says, "The works of his hands are truth and justice; all his instructions are trustworthy." God knows exactly what students and kids need, and He is able to hold them fast in the midst of very hard situations.

In the midst of trouble, we have hope. We have an anchor for our soul (Hebrews 6:19). We have an unchanging God who will hold us fast. When every circumstance is alarming, our God is steady.

You are secure.

2 SAMUEL 22:2-3a

The LORD is my rock, my fortress, and my deliverer, my God, my rock where I seek refuge.

ROMANS 8:31

What, then, are we to say about these things? If God is for us, who is against us?

HEBREWS 13:6

Therefore, we may boldly say, The Lord is my helper; I will not be afraid. What can man do to me?

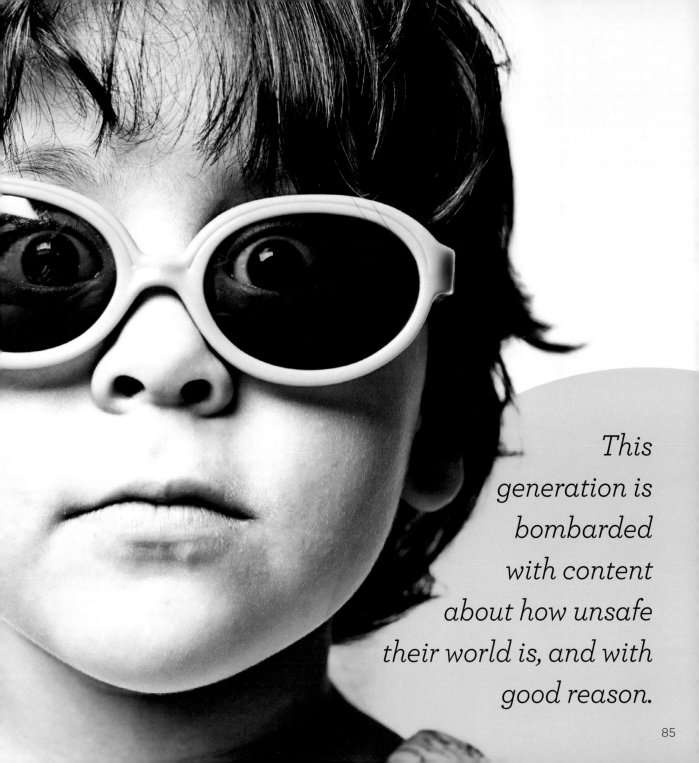

This generation is bombarded with content about how unsafe their world is, and with good reason.

GOD'S PLAN FOR MY LIFE

TRUTH #9—
I AM MADE FOR COMMUNITY

God never intended for you to be lonely, alone, or isolated.

God is a relational God. He exists as God the Father, God the Son, and God the Holy Spirit. Before the world began, community existed. Kids and students need to know that we are made for relationship because the Maker Himself exists in relationship. We are made to be connected to God and to other people in relationships: in friendships, in partnerships, in groups, on teams, in families, in communities, and in cultures.

God designed the church to be the center of biblical community. The church is meant to be a place where people find belonging. We need to help each child connect to his or her true identity as a forgiven son or daughter of God. We need to lead kids and students to realize that following Jesus means they have been adopted into God's family and knit into biblical community for an important purpose.

We are meant to encourage one another and build each other up. We're to love one another, care for one another, pray for one another, serve one another, cry with one another, carry one another's burdens, and celebrate with one another. We are meant to do life together with other people who love and follow Jesus. You are not meant to be alone.

You are made for community.

ROMANS 15:7 (ESV)

Therefore welcome one another as Christ has welcomed you, for the glory of God.

HEBREWS 10:24-25

And let us consider one another to provoke love and good works, not neglecting to gather together, as some are in the habit of doing, but encouraging each other, and all the more as you see the day approaching.

MATTHEW 22:37-40

He said to him, "Love the Lord your God with all your heart, with all your soul, and with all your mind. This is the greatest and most important command. The second is like it: Love your neighbor as yourself. All the Law and the Prophets depend on these two commands."

10

TRUTH #10—
I AM MEANT TO KNOW GOD

God is knowable, and He wants you to know Him.

God is not unknowable, impersonal, or mysterious. All people, including the kids and students you serve, have been designed to know God and be in a personal relationship with Him. He has placed inside each of them a need to know Him.

God has revealed Himself to us through His written Word, the Bible, and through the Living Word—Jesus. Through the Bible, we discover God's character, His attributes, His personality, and His heart. Jesus shows us God's power, His holiness, His faithfulness, and His loving-kindness through His life, ministry, and testimony. Both the written Word and the Living Word testify to the goodness of God—the kindness of God to His people in the past and the promises of God that are for us today.

Kids and students need to root their identities in God Himself— to know He doesn't just know them, but He wants to be known by them. God is living and active. He is involved in our lives and in the world today. He is working out His will in history and humanity for His glory. He has not taken a hands-off approach to the world we live in. God is with your kids and students today, and He is involved in the here-and-now of life.

Just like the people of the Bible knew God, we can know Him too. He is not far away. He has revealed Himself through His Word, and He wants us to know Him.

You are meant to know God.

JOHN 17:3

This is eternal life: that they may know you, the only true God, and the one you have sent—Jesus Christ.

PROVERBS 8:17b

… those who search for me find me.

2 PETER 3:18

But grow in the grace and knowledge of our Lord and Savior Jesus Christ. To him be the glory both now and to the day of eternity.

TRUTH #11—
I AM DESIGNED FOR A PURPOSE

You were designed to do good things for God's kingdom.

God is just and faithful. He sees the brokenness in His world and promises to make all things new one day. Until that time, He is working in His world through His people to further His plan and kingdom. The kids you reach are part of that plan. They are not random. They are not insignificant. They are designed for an important purpose.

Ephesians 2:10 tells us that we are "created in Christ Jesus for good works, which God prepared ahead of time for us to do." Kids need to know that their identities are created by God and their purpose on this planet was predetermined by God—to do good things in the world for His kingdom. He made students and kids exactly who they are and placed them exactly where they are to be His representatives for good in the broken world.

Their existence was planned by God. Students are not useless, meaningless, or purposeless. God has a divine and inspired plan for their lives.

God calls us His ambassadors (2 Corinthians 5:20). When we live our lives for Him, He promises to work in and through us. We are to live like Jesus lived: serving, loving, instructing, helping, healing, and ministering to people in their broken condition in our broken world.

You were designed by God for a purpose.

ISAIAH 1:17

Learn to do what is good. Pursue justice. Correct the oppressor. Defend the rights of the fatherless. Plead the widow's cause.

MICAH 6:8

Mankind, he has told each of you what is good and what it is the LORD requires of you: to act justly, to love faithfulness, and to walk humbly with your God.

EPHESIANS 2:10

For we are his workmanship, created in Christ Jesus for good works, which God prepared ahead of time for us to do.

12

MATTHEW 5:15-16

No one lights a lamp and puts it under a basket, but rather on a lampstand, and it gives light for all who are in the house. In the same way, let your light shine before others, so that they may see your good works and give glory to your Father in heaven.

MARK 16:15

Then he said to them, "Go into all the world and preach the gospel to all creation."

1 PETER 3:15

But in your hearts regard Christ the Lord as holy, ready at any time to give a defense to anyone who asks you for a reason for the hope that is in you.

TRUTH #12—
I AM HERE TO SHARE JESUS

You are here to tell others about Jesus.

God designed the purpose and plan for each person's core identity to be part of a movement of extravagant welcome and pointing others to the unending joy of knowing Jesus. The purpose of our lives as Christians is not to achieve success, attain fame, or gain riches, status, or power. There is one single overriding, all-consuming purpose for God's people—the reason they were created—that is at the heart of who we are as followers of Jesus—to share Jesus with other broken people who need to know Him.

Before He ascended into heaven Jesus gave His disciples the Great Commission. God's plan and passion of this commission was for these men to live into their identities to be disciples who made even more disciples, passing on the mission to generation after generation. The call of God is to come and see, then go and show. Come and hear, then go and tell. Come and get, then go and give. The joyful mandate of every believer—including kids and students—is to share Jesus with people who don't know Him so that they too can find their true identities in Christ.

The kids and students in your ministry are uniquely equipped to share Jesus with the people they know in the places they go. This is what we are made for. This is rooted in our identities as children of God.

You are here to share Jesus.

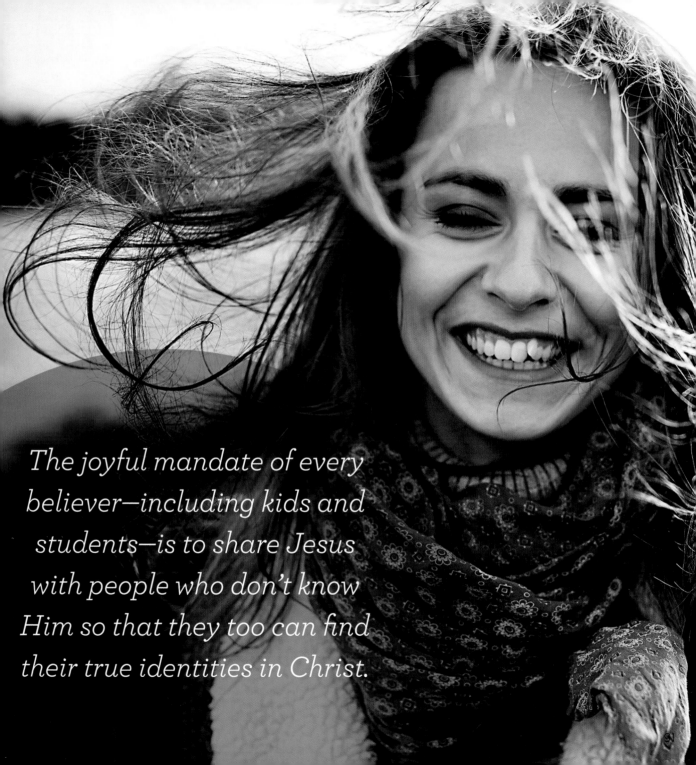

The joyful mandate of every believer—including kids and students—is to share Jesus with people who don't know Him so that they too can find their true identities in Christ.

IDENTITY FOUND

These 12 truths speak to the heart of our identity in Christ. Identity is not something that we determine or discover for ourselves; it's something that has already been authored by God. Because He made us who we are, He shows us who He intended for us to be in Jesus. As the church, we must be cautious to present these 12 truths in a way that makes them approachable and accessible to those who are new and uninitiated in the church. We must level the playing field for those who are not accustomed to Christian language and lingo, so they can easily understand that the message of the Bible is for them.

An added benefit is that when we present these rich truths in the language that's approachable to newcomers, kids and students who are already in the church will understand them as well.

This heart for the ones who are far from God is clear in the parables of Luke 15. As Jesus spoke of the lost sheep, the lost coin, and the lost son, He illustrated in each story a heart that is oriented to seek out, search out, and bring in the ones who are far and need to be found.

In the parable of the lost sheep we see the owner leaving behind the 99 who are safe to actively pursue the one who is far away from the fold. The sheep owner searches far and wide, tirelessly, to find his lost sheep. When he finds the lost lamb, he lifts it up, puts it on his shoulders, and carries it home.

It is noteworthy that the coin had been lost inside the house. This is a poignant reminder that there are many who may be inside our churches, attending on a regular basis, who are physically close in proximity to the gospel, but who may in fact be far from God spiritually. As with the sheep owner, the woman searched tenaciously for the one that was missing but inside the house. She swept, she shone a light, she did not rest until

God ... wants to give us a new identity. He wants to give us a new self, which is greater than a new reputation. A new identity that God gives us is not something we achieve but something that we freely receive.

—Derwin Gray

the one has been located and brought back to the place where it belonged.

In the story of the lost son, the heart of the father is evident. Jesus tells us that when the son was still a long way off, the father saw him. He had eyes to look up and look out for his son to return. He did not wait for the son to get all the way to the house, but when he saw him at a great distance, the father ran to him and embraced him. Although the son had prepared his response to the father, that he was no longer worthy to be a son but would like to be welcomed as a servant, the father had a different idea.

The response of the father is profound in light of the notion of our identity. Instead of offering his returning son a job, the father restored his true identity. The father told his servants to be quick, to bring the best robe, the ring, and sandals to put on his son's feet. These installments represent the placing of identity. And in placing them on him, the father, through a beautiful act of mercy and grace, declared him not a slave but his son. It wasn't his assessment of his own identity that mattered. It was the true identity that was given to him by his father.

In his mind, the son was not worthy of an identity in the family because of his past attitudes and actions. The son believed his identity had been lost. But the heart of the father saw the true value of the person before him, not because of what he had done, but because of who he was—his son. A son who was lost and had been found—a son who was dead but was alive again.

In every case, the response is the same: the search party turned into an actual party. In each situation, the searchers called together their friends and neighbors to celebrate. Jesus explained that likewise there is great rejoicing in heaven over everyone who comes to repentance. The church party should be a search party, and the search party should result in a church party!

The church has the opportunity and responsibility to teach people who God says they are, so each person can come to find his identity in Christ, where it is intended to be. It is not the identity that we choose for ourselves that matters. It is the identity that has been reserved for us by God that determines our true purpose and value in Him, to Him, and through Him.

Some of these truths are true for everyone—I am known, I am designed, and I am loved, for instance. Still others are fulfilled at the time of redemption and are only realized after a child or student trusts in Jesus for salvation—I am forgiven, I am secure, I am here to tell others about Jesus.

Wherever kids or students are on their spiritual journeys, we must remember that the truths we declare are only true for us because they are rooted in the truth of who God is. God is Designer and Creator. He is all-knowing, loving, forgiving, and desiring that all would come to salvation. This is what makes people valuable. Our value does not come from our culture, our status, or our abilities. Our value comes from who God says we are because of who He is. People can only know who they truly are when they know who God is.

5

FLIP THE SCRIPT:
A WHOLE-CHURCH STRATEGY

THIS MINISTRY PHILOSOPHY ISN'T JUST FOR KIDS!

We've looked at several strategies that can impact NextGen Ministries including radical hospitality, psychological safety, and building FLIP relationships. These strategies are pivotal toward creating a NextGen movement where kids and students see and know who they are because of who God is. But we as leaders cannot do this alone. The whole church needs to get behind these strategies to maximize the benefits for kids and students. As a church family, we need to circle around kids, students, and families through relationships.

While the majority of our focus thus far has been on strategies for kids and student ministries, these strategies can move beyond the bounds of NextGen Ministry to impact the whole church. The entire church benefits when it invests in building a church-wide culture of belonging.

STARTING POINTS

In chapter 2, we encouraged ministry leaders to stop assuming kids and students enter their ministry with a Christian worldview. We should challenge our assumptions on starting points with adults as well. While kids and students have been influenced by expressive individualism since birth, adults (especially in regions where secular thought has a deeper foothold) have been impacted as well. Churches need to assume that adults visiting church may not enter ready to hear the teaching.

We need to build an environment of radical hospitality, break down barriers to belonging, and help people engage with others before engaging them with teaching. This strategy creates the right environment for hearing and learning. The key to opening hearts to hear the gospel is relationships. The key to building strong, long-lasting volunteer teams is relationships. The key to discipling kids, students, families, and adults in your church is … you guessed it … relationships.

The entire church benefits when it invests in building a church-wide culture of belonging.

OUTSIDER-IN METHODOLOGY FOR THE CHURCH

Based on the falling church attendance statistics we saw in chapter 1, we can no longer assume that if we build it they will come. The post-Christian culture has lost confidence in the church as an institution, or worse, views the church with suspicion. Despite this, research from Lifeway Research for the Billy Graham Center for Evangelism shows that people are willing to come to all types of church-sponsored events, especially those that seem low-risk to a non-believer.

Unchurched Americans are more likely to accept an invitation to a church-sponsored neighborhood safety event, community service project, sports or exercise program, concert, or community meet-up.[28] These casual encounters allow people to build trust with the church as an institution and form relationships with church members who attend.

Remember the Outsider-In methodology recommended in chapter 3? (See pages 54-55.) The same can be applied to your community. People who have no connection to your church feel like outsiders. They need to feel a sense of psychological safety before they can move toward feeling included, then toward participation. Creating spaces for community events that feel low-risk (festivals, sports, neighborhood safety seminars, etc.) helps move people in your community toward inclusion. Once they begin to feel a level of connection, they are more likely to respond to a personal invitation to a holiday service, or small group cookout.

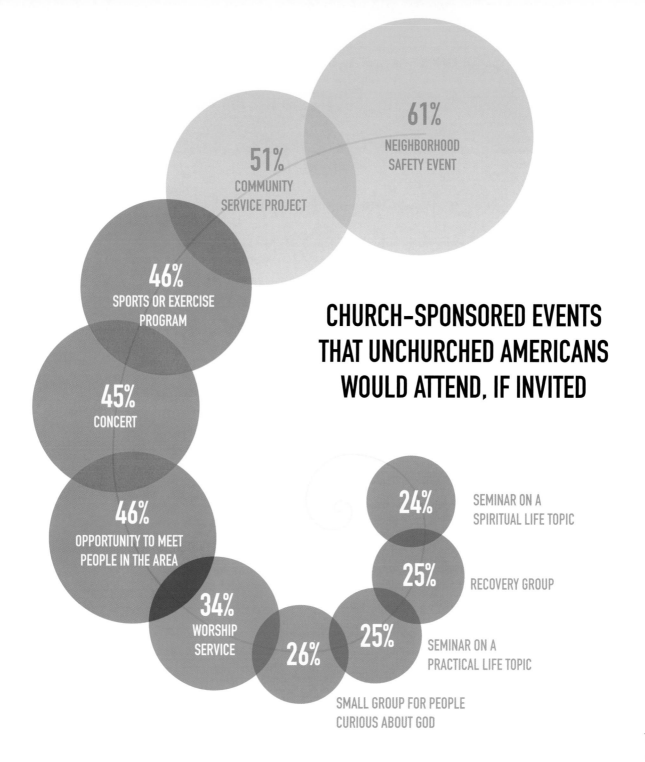

61%
NEIGHBORHOOD
SAFETY EVENT

51%
COMMUNITY
SERVICE PROJECT

46%
SPORTS OR EXERCISE
PROGRAM

45%
CONCERT

46%
OPPORTUNITY TO MEET
PEOPLE IN THE AREA

34%
WORSHIP
SERVICE

26%
SMALL GROUP FOR PEOPLE
CURIOUS ABOUT GOD

25%
SEMINAR ON A
PRACTICAL LIFE TOPIC

25%
RECOVERY GROUP

24%
SEMINAR ON A
SPIRITUAL LIFE TOPIC

CHURCH-SPONSORED EVENTS
THAT UNCHURCHED AMERICANS
WOULD ATTEND, IF INVITED

TRY THIS!

THINK CIRCLES, NOT ROWS

The ways that we arrange our chairs within the spaces we meet can enhance or impede the effectiveness of relational connections. As we try to build ministries that are founded on relationships, we find that circles are better than rows.

When chairs are organized in rows, everyone faces the same direction in a setting that is like a classroom at school. This seating arrangement is not conducive to personal interaction and connection. People in rows tend to spread out, leaving empty chairs between them and other people. This creates space that serves as a relational buffer. It limits eye contact and restricts opportunities to connect, engage, and interact with others. In row settings, content is typically communicated from the front of the room by a single leader. While there may be some opportunity for questions and discussion in this setting, they tend to be more formal in style. Listeners talk to the leader, not to one another, and participation requires people to be more bold and confident. It can be intimidating to speak up in front of a large group.

Rows are meant for listening to lectures.

Circles are more suited for relational ministry.

Circles are more conducive to engagement, interaction, communication, and participation in discussion. Circles keep people in closer proximity to one another. By their shape, circles discourage spreading out, so we come together. Circles make participants feel seen and included and cause people to feel more comfortable sharing their thoughts and observations.

Circles foster interactive discussion.

RELATIONSHIPS IN ROWS

How do people get plugged in and build relationships? In most churches, it looks something like this: kids are dropped off in kids ministry, while students head off to the student ministry wing. They may make a few friends and get to know their leader, to some extent. Often, that's the entire scope of their relationship network—a row of fairly lateral peer relationships—because some churches can be more focused on teaching people instead of connecting people. But research shows that newcomers aren't going to stick around to learn if they don't go deeper and wider in their relationships. In chapter 3, we saw that 70% of church kids stop attending regularly between ages 18–22, and most of the reasons given were relational.[29]

KID —— KID —— KID —— KID

STUDENT —— STUDENT —— STUDENT —— STUDENT

Adults and volunteers attending weekend services primarily have relationships with other adults. Volunteers are too busy serving on Sunday to get to know the other volunteers. They may be connected to the church enough to have some relationships with a few influencers in the church, but most of these adult relationships are fairly lateral as well.

LEADER —— ADULT —— LEADER —— ADULT

Every church has influencers. These might be longstanding members, church founders, influential families, or people who serve in multiple ministry areas. These influencers tend to have mostly lateral relationships with other influencers from serving on committees together.

INFLUENCER-INFLUENCER-INFLUENCER-INFLUENCER

Pastors tend to have strong relationships with each other and some key influencers, but they can't invest in every single person, right? There may be a few personal connections, but they are often weak. Even pastors' connections are mostly lateral.

PASTOR —— PASTOR —— PASTOR —— PASTOR

Are these lateral relationships enough to really connect people to one another? Gallup research shows that friendships with other church members is a key reason adults stay connected and grow at a church.[30] An environment of relationships in rows isn't enough to connect people to each other.

FLIP THE ROWS INSIDE OUT: MESSY AND BEAUTIFUL

We need to flip these rows inside out. Every person, regardless of age, longs to be known, seen, and wanted. Congregations thrive within cultures of connection. Kids, students, adults, volunteers, influencers, and pastors need a web of interconnected relationships with each other, not static rows of relationships with people in the same life stage or church role.

People in every stage of life struggle with loneliness and isolation. We are more "connected" than ever before, but evidence shows that virtual relationships through social media are not fulfilling or satisfying. They cannot meet the deep need that humans have for relational connection. While many people have hundreds (or thousands) of online "friends" and "followers," research shows that people are more emotionally isolated and feel lonelier than ever. However, social media does excel at fostering a network of interconnectivity with a diverse set of people, and we can learn from that. Replicating a diverse network with real connections with fellow believers in the local church knits congregations together. Discipleship happens in the context of relationships. Churches who focus on fostering interpersonal connections produce connections that nurture faith and encourage faithfulness.

Kids and students benefit from being known by parents other than their own. Influencers benefit from knowing students in the church. Pastors benefit from deep friendships with volunteers. These networks of relationships link us together. Flipping these relational rows inside out looks messier than straight rows of lateral relationships. Relationship-based ministry is messy because relationships are messy. But they are also beautiful, rich, and more reflective of our triune God. We discussed in chapter 3 the need for kids and students to experience relationships with friends, leaders, influencers, and pastors. But everyone in the church needs these FLIP relationships.

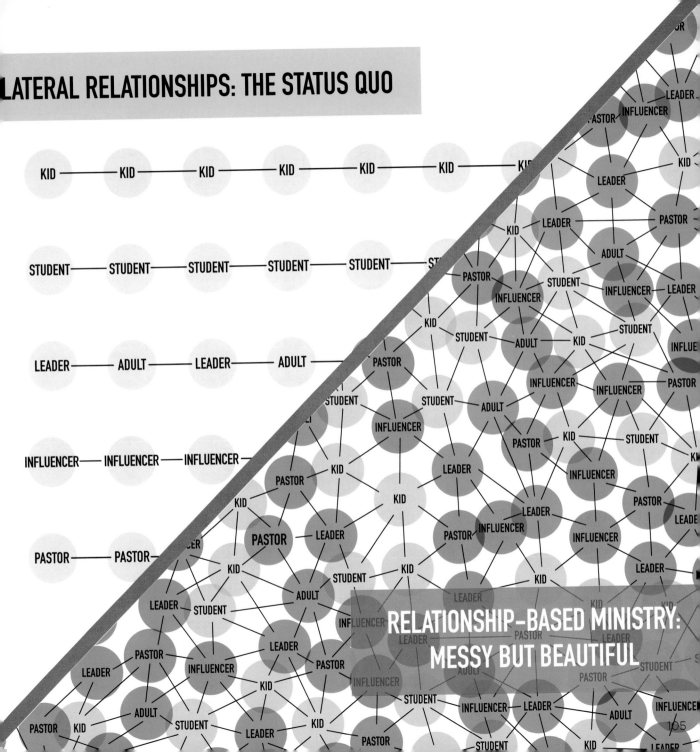

LATERAL RELATIONSHIPS: THE STATUS QUO

KID — KID — KID — KID — KID — KID — KID

STUDENT — STUDENT — STUDENT — STUDENT — STUDENT — ST

LEADER — ADULT — LEADER — ADULT —

INFLUENCER — INFLUENCER — INFLUENCER —

PASTOR — PASTOR —

RELATIONSHIP-BASED MINISTRY: MESSY BUT BEAUTIFUL

105

HAVING A BEST FRIEND IN THE SAME CONGREGATION HAS A SIGNIFICANT IMPACT ON SPIRITUAL LIFE

BEST FRIEND IN SAME CONGREGATION

BEST FRIEND NOT IN SAME CONGREGATION

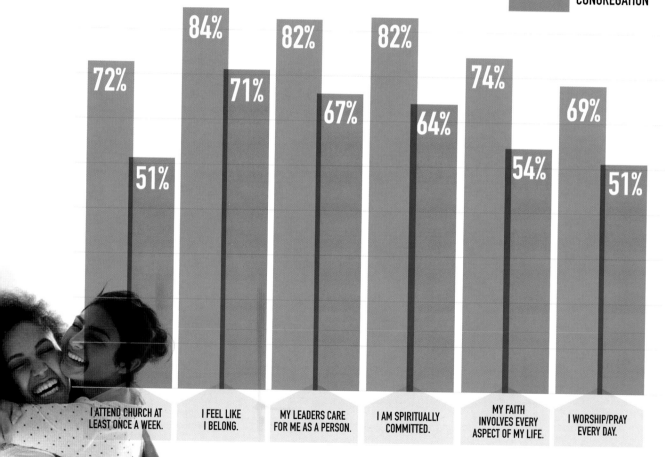

72%	84%	82%	82%	74%	69%
51%	71%	67%	64%	54%	51%
I ATTEND CHURCH AT LEAST ONCE A WEEK.	I FEEL LIKE I BELONG.	MY LEADERS CARE FOR ME AS A PERSON.	I AM SPIRITUALLY COMMITTED.	MY FAITH INVOLVES EVERY ASPECT OF MY LIFE.	I WORSHIP/PRAY EVERY DAY.

F RIENDS NEED FLIP RELATIONSHIPS

Kids and students aren't the only ones who benefit from finding friends at church. Friend relationships are vital to everyone. Leaders, influencers, and pastors need friend connections of their own. God created us to live in relationship. Relationships enrich our lives and create a platform for the hard work of sanctification. Research shows that adults who have a best friend in the same congregation attend church more often, feel a greater sense of belonging, are more spiritually committed, and worship/pray daily at a higher rate than those who do not.[31] Relationship-building ministry cannot be confined to kids and students. As a whole congregation, we have the opportunity to create on-ramps for kids, students, adults, families, leaders, and pastors to connect with each other. Here are a few ideas to get you started.

- **Provide opportunities for families to interact.** The parents in your church have at least one big thing in common—raising children. They are in similar seasons of life, depending on the age of each kid. Don't miss the opportunity to connect families with each other during this shared experience. When parents are friends, their kids are usually friends, which helps develop lasting relationships that make a difference.

- **Get more adults and students involved in kids ministry.** This is a challenge if every job requires expert teaching skills, so create volunteer roles that focus on relationship-building, encouragement, or game-leading. Help these leaders recognize that their role is to see, know, and love kids, and to be known by kids as a safe and trusted leader.

- **Make NextGen ministry the hub for planning family events.** Focus on having fun together and building friendships. Families who have ties to each other will become more strongly connected to the church. As those relationships grow, kids and students will begin to have "influencer" relationships with other parents, older kids, and students.

FRIENDSHIPS AT CHURCH ARE VITAL, BUT MANY ARE MISSING OUT

35% of churchgoers do not attend a class or small group.

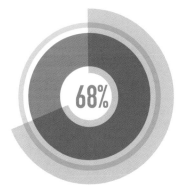

Of those who are not in a small group 68% are open to attending one, *but are not actively looking.*

If there is one thing parents need, it's the friendship of other parents in different seasons of parenting.

- **Find ways for students to serve.** Research shows that serving in church is one of the top predictors that a student will become a spiritually healthy young adult, so find places for students to serve on ministry teams. They can be influencers and leaders in kids ministry, VBS, or kids camp. They can serve on parking/hospitality teams where they will build relationships with influencers and leaders.

LEADERS NEED FLIP RELATIONSHIPS

All people in the church benefit when they have a leader who invests in them. Adult Bible study, Sunday School, and small group leaders are excellent connectors for the entire church.

Leaders need to be connected in meaningful relationships for their own benefit. They need to feel valued by friends, influencers, and pastors who are building relationships with them. Being a church leader can be relationally challenging. Who has time to build friendships at weekend services when you are busy volunteering? Leaders also richly profit from the relationships they build with kids. How often do you hear, "I learned more from the kids than they learned from me"? Leaders must be open to think differently, to move beyond a passion for the area in which they serve toward a passion for relational engagement. Here are some practical ideas for building a network of friends for leaders:

- **Prioritize creating community** within your volunteer team. Hold regular social events where they can build relationships with each other and as a team.
- **Encourage adult groups to serve** on ministry teams together.
- **Be intentional in finding ways to engage** with kids and students in adult small groups, such as sharing a group

meal or party at regular intervals. Doing this makes kids and students feel included and known.

- **Plan community service days** where everyone in the church can serve alongside one another: cleaning local schools, serving food to those in need, or volunteering for any service your community needs. This creates an environment for all age groups to go, serve, and tell others about Jesus alongside each other.

INFLUENCERS NEED FLIP RELATIONSHIPS

Influencers are relational connectors who tend to inspire or guide the actions of others. It may be easy for them to feel content with the relationships they've already established. It's more challenging to make time to meet the relational needs of others when your personal need in that area is already met. Pursuing new relationships that extend influence outside of current circles is a way to serve others that will enrich kids and students as well. Influencers of all ages may be the key to helping the ministry of biblical belonging become a church-wide movement.

The church can never have too many people who inspire others to look to Jesus. Everyone in the church can connect with other people as an influencer in some way; people just need to be encouraged to think of themselves as someone who can point others towards spiritual growth. Here are some practical ideas for helping add new influencers and growing the relational networks of current influencers:

- **Seek out potential influencers** church-wide and challenge them to invest in others. These may be kids, students, or adults. Encourage them to lead the charge in seeking out newcomers/infrequent attendees and extending an extravagant welcome.

- **Establish ministry teams and committees** not only to get work done but also as a way to build another layer of community. Offer servant leaders ways to connect and build relationships outside of the current responsibilities they do for the church. It's easy to drop out of serving when you are just there to do a job. But when people feel truly connected to those they are serving with—when those people become "their people"—they will stay for the long haul.

PASTORS RECOGNIZE THE NEED FOR FRIENDSHIP

69%

"Friendship and fellowship with others" is one of the top five issues pastors recognize as a ministry/personal need.

P ASTORS NEED FLIP RELATIONSHIPS

Leading the church can be relationally lonely. Pastors might struggle to build relationships with congregants because relationships require vulnerability and being known can be a risk. But pastors will find that relationships with kids, students, leaders, and influencers can both feed them and feed the congregation. Pastors can lead FLIP thinking from the pulpit. What can your pastors do to foster this kind of culture? Here are some practical ideas for encouraging your pastors to embrace the FLIP mindset and foster relationships outside of rows:

- **The pastor is the one person** who has the power to rally the whole church behind events like VBS, camp, and community service days, where all ages come together to build relationships and grow together.
- **Pastors can thank the influencers** in the church who do unnoticed jobs.
- **Pastors can encourage staff and volunteers** to prioritize relationship-building events.

People in all these groups need relationships with friends, leaders, influencers, and pastors to be truly connected to your church. The more cross-pollination you can create so that people can interact and get to know one another, the stronger these ties will be.

EVERY KID KNOWN BY NAME: A CHURCH-WIDE CHALLENGE

How do we rally the whole church around making kids and students feel known? What's a practical way the entire church can begin to create networks of relationships that include kids and students? We start by knowing their names. It may sound obvious, but the reality is that while most adults would say they care about the next generation, they don't actually know their names.

"Remember that a person's name is, to that person, the sweetest and most important sound in any language." —Dale Carnegie, author

When children hear their names, they feel wanted. They feel like they belong. They feel known. Ultimately, we want kids to know they are known by God. He knows their names and as a church, we should know their names too.

What would it look like if every adult at church knew every kid and student by name? If we can rally around building campaigns, recruiting volunteers, and starting new programs, then we should be able to rally around this one simple mission: Every Kid Known by Name.

Here are some ideas for implementing: Make banners that hang in high-traffic areas. Announce the challenge from the stage/pulpit. Make social media posts. Provide name tags to wear each week. Pair adult small groups with small groups in the kids and student ministries. Have all church staff model how to do this.

"Every Kid Known by Name" can be scalable regardless of the church size. The point is not to start and finish a campaign. The point is to build a culture that normalizes calling one another by name and to intentionally know the next generation of preschoolers, kids, and students.

A SIGNIFICANT PORTION OF THE CONGREGATION CONNECTS TO NEXTGEN MINISTRY IN SOME WAY.

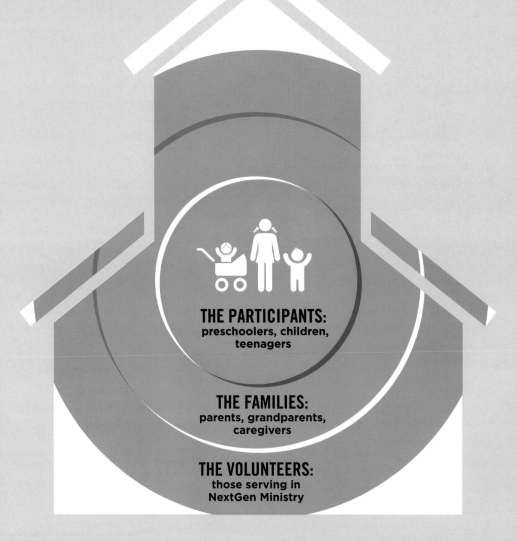

THE PARTICIPANTS:
preschoolers, children, teenagers

THE FAMILIES:
parents, grandparents, caregivers

THE VOLUNTEERS:
those serving in NextGen Ministry

MAKE RELATIONSHIP-RICH ENVIRONMENTS THE CENTRAL HUB OF YOUR CHURCH

Why are our church relationships stuck in lateral rows? For most churches, the weekly worship service serves as the central focus of the church, and all other ministries are secondary. But the weekend service is one of the least relationship-rich environments in the church. We sit in rows with little interaction. God created us to worship Him individually and in community. It is important to worship with your local church gathered around God's Word and praising Him together. But we are not truly doing so in community if we don't know the people around us.

What if we flipped the paradigm to first invite people to any place where people interact—places like kids or student ministries, small groups, or ministry teams? These are the places where people will become truly connected to each other and to the church. The stronger these connections are, the more likely people are to make faith a part of every aspect of their lives.

What would it look like for NextGen ministries to be at the center of belonging at church? People with ties to NextGen ministry make up a significant portion of the entire church congregation! There are three big groups of people represented in a typical kids or student ministry.

- **The Participants:** preschoolers, children, teenagers
- **The Families**: parents, grandparents, caregivers
- **The Volunteers:** those serving in NextGen ministry

How do we make sure that these groups feel like they are known and that they belong? No pressure, but it begins with you—the ministry leader! While most churches strive to promote the value of biblical community through Sunday School classes and small groups, many are missing the opportunity to leverage the power of a common denominator. That common denominator could be our NextGen ministries.

FRIENDSHIP IS BORN AT THAT MOMENT WHEN ONE PERSON SAYS TO ANOTHER: "WHAT? YOU TOO? I THOUGHT I WAS THE ONLY ONE!"

—C.S. LEWIS

Families need to feel connected to the ministries their children are attending. Too many times, parents drop off their kids and pick them up without ever knowing their kids' leaders, their friends, or the other parents. This is a missed opportunity for building belonging at church. The number one thing families have in common is the season of life they find themselves in while parenting children of the same age group. Ministry leaders have the ability to connect these families during a time where conversations can naturally occur and connections can easily be made. The church has an opportunity, if not an obligation, to come alongside parents and walk together with them as partners in the spiritual formation and development of their children through kids and student ministries.

Volunteers need to be connected to one another. Volunteers who feel a sense of belonging to the group and a real connection with kids will discover how much they love volunteering and stay for the long haul. Create volunteer roles that can focus on relationship-building with kids. Plan events that connect volunteers to each other so they become a linked community. Volunteers who feel connected to each other have a stronger connection to the church.

When we make relationship-based groups the central hub of the church, the weekend service can become the tie that binds these relationship-rich environments together. We can leverage the weekly service to help the whole church family connect. Thinking like this starts us on the path to helping people grow the number of their connections.

THE CHURCH IS MADE FOR COMMUNITY

Relationship-focused ministry is messy and difficult to execute, but if we can make the FLIP, then we will see more kids and students stay and more families plug into the life of the church. We can't continue along the path of 66% of kids and students leaving the church when they become young adults. Kids and students are 100% of the future of the church!

The early church lived in close relational proximity. They cared for those in need and gave generously to one another. They walked together, ate together, studied the Scriptures together, and reasoned together. Teaching took place in the context of relationships. They met in their homes and experienced life together. Following Jesus didn't just mean believing in the person of Jesus or studying His teachings, it included joining a community of faith. The early church found their identity in Jesus and lived out that identity with other believers.

Many churches today have largely lost their sense of communal identity. The church is more likely to reflect the individualism of culture than the value of community found in the Bible.[32] Many church attenders do not feel a true sense of belonging in their churches. That's not how the church was intended to function.

What if we cast a different vision for our churches? What if our churches were places that were built on a foundation of biblical belonging in Christ-centered community? What if our churches were devoted to the demonstration of extreme welcome and radical hospitality, where everyone who entered felt seen, noticed, and known? Imagine a church where every member was trained to have eyes that see and recognize newcomers; where people know that they are missed when they're away and that they're celebrated when they return. How might this kind of culture change our churches?

The strategy of belonging could be a game changer for the church, but for the strategy to succeed, it needs to be championed at our highest levels of leadership. When pastors and church leaders champion a culture of belonging for the whole church, the whole church will benefit—and the overflow will impact our neighborhoods, communities, and cities for the sake of the gospel.

ABOVE ALL, MAINTAIN CONSTANT LOVE FOR ONE ANOTHER, SINCE LOVE COVERS A MULTITUDE OF SINS. BE HOSPITABLE TO ONE ANOTHER WITHOUT COMPLAINING. JUST AS EACH ONE HAS RECEIVED A GIFT, USE IT TO SERVE OTHERS, AS GOOD STEWARDS OF THE VARIED GRACE OF GOD.

—1 PETER 4:8-10

CONCLUSION

WE MUST HELP KIDS AND STUDENTS FIND THEIR TRUE IDENTITIES IN CHRIST

Heart transformation, identity change, and redemption come only through the person and work of Jesus, so Jesus, must be clear and present in our ministries. Everything we do should serve to point to Jesus and help kids and students know Him personally. Bold conversations about the gospel should be a regular part of our ministries. It should not be difficult to see Jesus in our ministries.

We should always seek to celebrate and elevate the name of Jesus Christ, God's Son, our Savior, the Messiah, and the hope of salvation He offers. Jesus is the author and finisher of our faith. He is Immanuel, God with us. He became the sacrifice for our sins. In Him we find forgiveness for sins. There is no longer any condemnation for those who are found in Christ Jesus. He sets us free from the laws of sin and death. He has removed our sin "(as) far as the east is from the west" (Psalm 103:12).

Jesus is the one and only mediator between God and man. (See 1 Timothy 2:5.) He is the way, the truth, and the life; no one can come to the Father except through Jesus. (See John 14:6.) Acts 4:12 declares, "There is salvation in no one else, for there is no other name under heaven given to people by which we must be saved."

Everything that exists was created through Him and for Him. (See Colossians 1:16.) Every breath we breathe is given by Him. (See Acts 17:25.) Every good thing we have is provided by Him. (See James 1:17.) One day, every knee will bow, and "every tongue will confess that Jesus Christ is Lord, to the glory of God the Father" (Philippians 2:10-11).

He is the solution to our sin problem. He is the spotless lamb, the promised Messiah, the Good Shepherd, our Savior, Redeemer and King. Jesus is the head of the church and the reason for the church. The Bible is one big story that is all about Him. He should be the reason for everything we do. It's all about Jesus.

HOLD TIGHTLY TO JESUS, NOT MINISTRY MODELS

We should always cling tightly to the timeless things that matter: biblical teaching that points to Jesus, sound doctrine, life application, and heart transformation. And we should discipline ourselves to hold our teaching methods with a loose grip. As leaders and teachers, we must be willing to meet the needs of those we teach with flexibility in our ministry models. Each generation will respond to different methods and ministry models, depending on the cultural influences of the day. Understanding those influences can help us build the right environment that will serve kids and students to develop an openness to hear and respond to the good news of Jesus. It can be challenging for long-time teachers and leaders to adjust our methods to meet the needs of new generations, but it will pay great dividends!

We can't keep standing on the outside of the fishbowl instructing fish how to walk. Kids and students today aren't going to trust anyone speaking at them through a warped fishbowl glass. Dive in! Plunge into relationships! Ask questions about their starting points, what they believe, and why. Never water down the message of Christ, but first make sure kids and students know you care for them deeply so you earn the right to be heard. Assume all kids and students arrive feeling like outsiders, and do everything you can to make them feel like they belong. Help kids and students form FLIP relationships so they have many voices pointing them to Jesus! Counter their fishbowl worldview by soaking them in biblical truth—that who they are is defined by who God is.

POSTSCRIPT:
WHAT WE TEACH MATTERS

WHAT WE TEACH MATTERS

As we evaluate the effectiveness of our ministry strategies and consider the adaptation of new methods to reach those who are far from God, we must be careful not to make the mistake of believing that the method we use is all that matters. Yes, there is merit in thinking that we might multiply the impact and influence of our ministries by creating a culture of relational connection that builds a sense of biblical belonging, but in doing so we must not lose sight of the truth that what we teach remains extremely important.

Scripture is clear that those who teach God's Word to others, even those who teach children, will be held accountable for the content and concepts they convey.

James 3:1 and Matthew 18:6 are warnings that we must take seriously as spiritual leaders.

> *"Not many should become teachers, my brothers, because you know that we will receive a stricter judgment." James 3:1*

> *"But whoever causes one of these little ones who believe in me to fall away—it would be better for him if a heavy millstone were hung around his neck and he were drowned in the depths of the sea." Matthew 18:6*

Considering these warnings, we as leaders need to take great care in evaluating what we are teaching inside our churches. This includes, but is not limited to, the content of the curriculum we use. We cannot shirk or neglect this responsibility considering our future accountability. Let's be assured that the content we teach is not just fun but is also biblically sound, doctrinally trustworthy, and age appropriate.

WE MUST TEACH THE BIBLE

Research that the Lifeway Kids team published in the 2019 book *Nothing Less* by Jana Magruder identified childhood Bible reading as the #1 indicator of spiritual maturity in adulthood.[33] This means that if we can run a session in our ministry without opening a Bible, we are doing it wrong. If we want our ministries to produce kids and students who become spiritually mature adults, we must teach them to open, read, and study their Bibles.

The content we teach in our kids and student ministries must be built and based on the Bible. Examine your curriculum to make sure that it is actually and accurately based on biblical truth. Kids, students, leaders, and parents need to know that the things taught in our churches actually come from the Bible. While this may seem obvious, we cannot assume that it is the case.

Kids and students need to see that God's words come from God's book. We can demonstrate this by using a physical Bible when we teach or lead groups. Why? Because students and kids need to learn that God's book is the place to look to find God's truth, now and when they are older.

Let's be leaders who celebrate and elevate God's Word.

WE MUST TEACH SOUND DOCTRINE

We need to use care to make sure we are teaching doctrines that are solid and sound. It is sometimes necessary to simplify complex concepts when teaching young children, but we need to be cautious not to oversimplify to the point that what we teach is no longer biblical. Or that in simplifying we water-down the Word in ways that inadvertently introduce harmful heresies that can undermine a life of faith.

It can be easy for a well-meaning leader to inadvertently introduce heretical ideas when attempting to simplify complex biblical concepts to make them more understandable to children.

Too many people who work with kids brush off or reject concerns like this because they are "only teaching children." This is a dangerous response. It is extremely important that we teach foundational doctrines correctly. Considering the warnings in James 3:1 and Matthew 18:6, we cannot take lightly our responsibility to teach the Bible accurately, regardless of the age of our pupils. We must use care to ensure that we are not doing harm as we seek to do good.

In truth, there are many things about God that we simply cannot understand easily. For example, it is better to tell children that God the Father, Son, and Holy Spirit existing as a Trinity is a mystery that is hard for humans to understand than to give a simplistic answer that is incorrect.

We must teach sound doctrine.

WE MUST TEACH HEARING AND DOING

The work you do in preschool, kids, and student ministries lays a foundation for the current and future faith of each child in your church. Is the foundation being built soft or strong? We must be faithful to lay foundations that are solid so that, on them, kids can build secure, mature faith that will last and hold strong.

The parable of the two foundations in Matthew 7 isn't really about building houses. Jesus used wise and foolish builders as examples of the two ways that people might respond to His teaching: those who acted on what they heard Him teach would be like the wise builder, and those who chose to ignore what they had heard would be like the foolish man.

This parable is about those who hear God's Word and do what it says. We need to teach the children under our instruction to both listen and act on God's Word. (James 1:22)

We must not teach things that cause kids and students to wrongly believe that discipleship is merely hearing. We must likewise not teach them that being a Christian is only doing. Therefore, we must teach them what the Bible says and instruct them in how they are to respond.

True discipleship requires both hearing and doing ... and more.

Our kids and students need to know that being a Christian isn't merely about:
- what you know (the head)
- what you do or don't do (the hands)
- the right words to say (the tongue)

Being a Christian is about:
- transformation (your heart)
- becoming like Jesus (your likeness)
- who you are (your identity in Christ)

Kids and students need to know that being a Christian isn't about increasing their understanding, changing their thinking, or altering their habits. At its core, being a Christian is merely about becoming a whole new person; it's about receiving an entirely new identity—one that is given by God and found in His Son, Jesus.

WE MUST REACH THE HEART

God has a lot to say about our hearts. Your heart reveals who you truly are; your authentic self. Everything you do flows from your heart. (Proverbs 4:23) The things you treasure reveal where your heart is. (Matthew 6:21) You can see into the character of a person's heart by how he lives. Isaiah 29:13 tells us that God sees through our lip service and heartless actions. God isn't satisfied with empty words or empty actions; He wants our hearts.

When asked what the Greatest Commandment was, Jesus echoed the words of the Shema from Deuteronomy 6:5, "Love the Lord your God with all your heart, with all your soul, with all your mind, and with all your strength" (Mark 12:30). His answer is recorded in Matthew 22:37; Mark 12:30; and Luke 10:27. In every recorded instance, Jesus always mentioned the heart first. Our heart matters to God. (See also 1 Samuel 16:7.)

Ezekiel tells us that God is in the business of giving His people new hearts. "I will give you a new heart and put a new spirit in you; I will remove from you your heart of stone and give you a heart of flesh" (Ezekiel 36:26).

As we train up our children in the ways of the Lord (see Ephesians 6:4), we must not merely teach them Bible facts and coach them to perform righteous acts. We need to disciple them to love God from the very depths of their inner beings, that they may be transformed into the image and likeness of Jesus.

INFOGRAPHICS:

CHAPTER 1:

p. 10

Aaron Earls, "Reaching the Unchurched Generations," Lifeway Research, April 1, 2022, https://research.lifeway.com/2022/04/01/reaching-the-unchurched-generations/.

p. 11

Harper Lee, *To Kill a Mockingbird* (London, England: Arrow, 2020), Chapter 3.

p. 12

Pew Research Center, "In U.S., Decline of Christianity Continues at Rapid Pace," Pew Research Center's Religion & Public Life Project (Pew Research Center, June 9, 2020), https://www.pewresearch.org/religion/2019/10/17/in-u-s-decline-of-christianity-continues-at-rapid-pace/.

p. 13

Pew Research Center, "In U.S., Decline of Christianity Continues at Rapid Pace," Pew Research Center's Religion & Public Life Project (Pew Research Center, June 9, 2020), https://www.pewresearch.org/religion/2019/10/17/in-u-s-decline-of-christianity-continues-at-rapid-pace/.

p. 14

Jeffrey M. Jones, "U.S. Church Membership Falls below Majority for First Time," Gallup.com (Gallup, November 20, 2021), https://news.gallup.com/poll/341963/church-membership-falls-below-majority-first-time.aspx.

p. 15

Charles Taylor, *A Secular Age* (Cambridge, MA: The Belknap Press of Harvard University Press, 2007), p. 3.

p. 16

Graphic 1:

Daniel A. Cox, "Generation Z and the Future of Faith in America," The Survey Center on American Life, March 24, 2022, https://www.americansurveycenter.org/research/generation-z-future-of-faith/.

Graphic 2:

Aaron Earls, "Reaching the Unchurched Generations," Lifeway Research, April 1, 2022, https://research.lifeway.com/2022/04/01/reaching-the-unchurched-generations/.

p. 17

Jill Nelson, "Who Is Catechizing Your Children?," Truth78 (Truth78, September 2, 2021), https://www.truth78.org/blog/post/who-is-catechizing-your-children.

p. 18

Mark Sayers, *Disappearing Church: From Cultural Relevance to Gospel Resilience* (Chicago, IL: Moody Publishers, 2016).

p. 20

Aaron Earls, "Americans' Theological Beliefs Changed to Suit Post-Pandemic Practice," Lifeway Research, September 19, 2022, https://research.lifeway.com/2022/09/19/americans-theological-beliefs-changed-to-suit-post-pandemic-practice/.

p. 21

Barna Group, "The Most Post-Christian Cities in America: 2019," Barna Group, June 5, 2019, https://www.barna.com/research/post-christian-cities-2019/.

p. 22

Graphic 1 ("Who Is Gen Z?")

Tracy Francis and Fernanda Hoefel, "'True Gen': Generation Z and Its Implications for Companies," McKinsey & Company (McKinsey & Company, February 4, 2022), https://www.mckinsey.com/industries/consumer-packaged-goods/our-insights/true-gen-generation-z-and-its-implications-for-companies.

Graphic 2 ("Mental Health Snapshots")

Jamieson Taylor and Kevin Singer, "Gen Z Mental Health Crisis: How Pastors Can Make A Difference," Lifeway Research, June 20, 2022, https://research.lifeway.com/2022/06/20/gen-z-mental-health-crisis-how-pastors-can-make-a-difference/.

Graphic 2b ("More than Half")

Sarah Berger, "Gen Z Is the Loneliest Generation, Survey Reveals, but Working Can Help," CNBC (CNBC, May 14, 2018), https://www.cnbc.com/2018/05/02/cigna-study-loneliness-is-an-epidemic-gen-z-is-the-worst-off.html.

Graphic 3 ("My Mental Health is Fair to Poor")

GEN X, MILLENNIALS, AND GEN Z

Sophie Bethune, "Gen Z More Likely to Report Mental Health Concerns," Monitor on Psychology (American Psychological Association, January 2019), https://www.apa.org/monitor/2019/01/gen-z.

SILENT GENERATION AND BABY BOOMERS

American Psychological Association, "Stress in America - American Psychological Association," October 2018, https://www.apa.org/news/press/releases/stress/2018/stress-gen-z.pdf.

Graphic 4 ("Gen Z Feels Stress About the News")

American Psychological Association, "Stress in America - American Psychological Association," October 2018, https://www.apa.org/news/press/releases/stress/2018/stress-gen-z.pdf.

p. 23

Taryn Finley and Zeba Blay, "9 Quotes from Zendaya That Remind Us Just How Awesome She Is," HuffPost (HuffPost, September 1, 2015), https://www.huffpost.com/entry/9-quotes-from-zendaya-that-remind-us-just-how-awesome-she-is_n_55e5c1eee4b-0b7a9633a3c9c.

p. 24

Whitney Houston, Debra Martin Chase, and Mario Iscovich (Producers), & Gary Marshall (Director), 2004. *The Princess Diaries 2: Royal Engagement* [Motion Picture]. United States: Walt Disney Pictures.

Casey Lewis, "Kristen Stewart Would like Us All to Stop Trying to Define Her Sexuality." Teen Vogue. Teen Vogue, August 12, 2015. https://www.teenvogue.com/story/kristen-stewart-on-sexuality#:~:text=%E2%80%9CGoogle%20me%2C%20I'm,I%20am%20an%20actress%2C%20man.

Darla K. Anderson (Producer) and Lee Unkrich, Adrian Molina (Directors), 2017. *Coco* [Motion Picture]. United States: Disney PIXAR.

Robert Lopez and Kristen Anderson-Lopez, "Let It Go." Walt Disney Records, 2013. https://genius.com/Idina-menzel-let-it-go-lyrics.

Geoff Johns and Ivan Reis, *Blackest Night, Volume 8* (New York, NY: DC Comics, 2010).

Magdalena, "GG Magree Unveils a New Rock-Infused Single Titled 'Deja Reve,'" CelebMix, March 22, 2022, https://celebmix.com/gg-magree-unveils-a-new-rock-infused-single-titled-deja-reve/.

p. 25

Ang Lee, Ping Dong, Li-Kong Hsu, William Kong (Producers) and Ang Lee (Director), 2000. *Crouching Tiger, Hidden Dragon* [Motion Picture]. United States: Columbia Pictures, Sony Pictures Classics.

Jerry Weintraub (Producer) & John G. Avildsen (Director), 1984. *The Karate Kid* [Motion Picture]. United States: Sony Pictures Entertainment.

Teen Blurb, "10 Motivational PewDiePie Quotes," Medium (Medium, August 17, 2020), https://teenblurb.medium.com/10-motivational-pewdiepie-quotes-581d647a6a5f.